Ventral Depths

Alchemical Themes and Mythic Motifs of

the Great Central Valley of California

Craig Chalquist, PhD

Book Two of the *Animate California Trilogy*

World Soul Books
worldsoulbooks.com

Printed in the United States of America
ISBN 978-0-9826279-3-8

Front cover photograph by Marc Crumpler.

Table of Contents

The Animate California Trilogy

The capacity to exploit and destroy entire landscapes has loomed in step with the loss of the sense of the world as alive and ensouled. We will not appreciate or protect what we do not love, have not gotten to know in depth, and cannot perceive apart from our industrially amplified cravings to conquer or consume.

The Animate California Trilogy offers heartfelt and reflectively researched studies, sketches, and experiential snapshots that behold the land of California not as an object to be marked off, measured out, or used up, but as a living subject worthy of understanding, safeguarding, and care. To that end the focus lingers with stories, images, and recurring motifs that join this fabled and edgy land, in sickness and in health, to the "inner" life of its inhabitants.

World Soul Books hopes that by introducing and illustrating the "personhood" of the Golden State, the Animate California Trilogy will invite the reader into richer contact with the subjectivity of the land, its creatures, its sea, its sky, and even the matter composing them. In the end, perhaps we are only as humane as we choose to cherish and feel at home in the places that nurture us.

ACKNOWLEDGMENTS

Thanks be to Kathryn Quick for acquainting me with Gold Country and helping me understand it and other Valley places in greater depth.

Thanks also to David "Mas" Masumoto and Gerald Haslam for information and, beyond that, decades of heartfelt and soulful literary illumination of the Valley; to Nicole Celaya, Joan Bewley, and many others for sharing how it was to grow up in the Valley; and to Lola McCrary (visit LolaCanHelp.com) for her critical thoughts and impressions about the first draft of this book.

DEDICATION

To Aphrodite, for awakening me from a slumber.

Into the Belly of Queen Calafia

Which is the true California? That is what we all wonder.

— Joan Didion, "Notes from a Native Daughter"

What a pain in the ass! I thought once sleep had begun to fade.

I had previously withstood reproaches brought by two insistent dreams; but who can say no to Aphrodite?

Even when she is being pissy. "It amazes me," she stated with an uncharacteristic frown as I admired the gold glint in her hair, "that your species is the bridge between Us and the diatoms." "Us" being the gods, or, in Jungian, deep psychic structures expressing themselves in personified form, thereby reconnecting personal consciousness to its imaginal and cultural foundations.

In the dream I had sighed. *You're telling me.*

By the time November takes a firm grip on the East Bay, most of the summer's heat has dissipated from Northern California. Clouds of deep sunset pink shade upward into magenta, then on into chilly, star-dotted blackness lit pearly white by the moon rising in the east. With such an evening now gone into morning, I lay beneath a comforter as pale light leaked in through the window blinds. "Dimelo," Aphrodite had called herself in the dream: "Tell It To Me." But my

1

first association was to Dimela, the daughter of Miles Teg, a fictional general in Frank Herbert's *Dune* novels. Seasoned by long service,
Teg had not wanted to be called out of retirement; but when he had
reluctantly donned his old uniform, he left his farm in the care of
Dimela and her husband. This time when I sighed the sun was up.

As an introvert, I tend to respond to outer clamor by either div-
ing into its heart or, more frequently, eagerly retiring from it. This
was one of those times when retirement summoned me in desirable,
slumberous hues. Maples still wore crimson colors, but birches
stood bare from shedding golden leaves that crunched beneath my
feet during evening walks, each step unlocking a pleasant earthy-
bitter odor. At home, my armchair, a candle, hot tea, and a pile of the
Western classics awaited...until dreams came calling to disrupt my
domestic fantasies.

I wrote *Deep California* and then *The Tears of Llorona* after years
spent listening in on the ecological complexes of the mission cities
and counties of California. This, I had decided, was preferable to
thirty-five years of acting them out unconsciously. And what is an
ecological complex?

When I moved to Contra Costa County after living for so many
years along the coast of the Golden State, I felt like I had driven into
a dream. Some I spoke with had trouble understanding why I had
moved away from the verdancy of western Sonoma County, with its
ranches and vineyards and cow pastures, down into the suburban
East Bay inland of the Caldecott Tunnel. ("From Eden to Erebus," I
remarked to friends and colleagues.) I moved to be closer to the
campus where I taught my graduate students, but I was also mor-
tally weary from years of deep research along El Camino Real, and
my intuition said Walnut Creek felt good for recuperation even
though the logic of this evaded me.

Shortly after moving into a detached rental off mythically named
Olympic Boulevard, I began to notice a pattern emerging like an
obscure symbol caught from a vaguely recalled dream. Out walking
one day in my new neighborhood, I kept finding myself in cul-de-
sacs. They were ubiquitous. Soon I passed a funeral parlor, and, a
few miles away, a Trident Society where a loved one's ashes could

be cremated. A sign told me that a home care business occupied the same building: "We Care." At the top of that street, a guarded retirement community named Rossmoor kept an ambulance busy: I would see its red lights or hear its sirens racing up there almost daily. At the nearby Safeway supermarket, most of the shoppers looked seventy-five or older. "I'm glad there are *some* gentlemen left," exclaimed a white-haired woman as she accepted a box I retrieved from a shelf beyond her reach.

Culturally, this part of California, blocked by the Oakland Hills from the cosmopolitan buzz of the coast, felt self-isolating in its flag-displaying, putter-wielding, sidewalk-watering conservatism. The Byron Park Retirement Center up the road looked like a castle, its four-storied wings flanked by baileys at the corners. People streaming through the shopping arcade that served as a downtown spoke as though living on an island apart from "liberals" and other wild beasts ranging somewhere beyond the lawns and parks. At an intersection an elderly pedestrian with a Ronald Reagan haircut asked me why I wasn't wearing a bicycle helmet. A neighbor who refused to acknowledge my waves stared narrowly at my beard as though it hid something unpatriotic; another neighbor kept decorative Halloween lights on until Christmas, and her Christmas lights on until they turned green on St. Patrick's Day. At night I often saw large, four-door American cars waddling without lights down tree-lined streets. Up the highway in the Carquinez Strait, a "Ghost Fleet" of rusting warships left over from World War II rode at anchor while waiting patiently to be moved somewhere else.

Many mythologies from around the world harbor tales of lost lands of timelessness and dream: Other Places where people leave the daily track, disembark, forget the passage of time, and perhaps go gently to sleep. "Contra Costa" can be translated "Opposite Coast," but *contra* also means "contrary to" or "Other." The Other Coast: a study in Otherworld mythology, a kind of Avalon or Fortunate Isle (*Fortunatae Insulae*) of apples and grains and fertile fields like those we tended in our demonstration garden located near (where else) Shadelands. So rich were these mineral-packed clay-loam soils once amended with compost that our peas and grasses grew straight through the winter, when turnips and beets actually popped from the ground as though overeager for harvesting. Just as water separated Avalon and the Isle of the Fortunate from the mainland, so San Francisco Bay separated us, like the hills, from the famous spired city and its upward-thrusting peninsula.

However, Otherworlds of blessed hills and vales often sit next door to sinister Underworlds: shadowy nightmare realms in which the decayed and the hellish collect in great dark pools of misery. In Hercules, for example, where decades of dynamite plant explosions once recalled the Greek hero's fiery death, a muscular husband killed his wife in 2010 by striking her with a dumbbell.

A few miles southwest of Hercules, Richmond, whose name means "Strong Hill," is a site of immense oil refineries, tanks laid out like pillboxes guarding the hills, and decades of chemical warfare quietly conducted against the land. Refineries here—such as Chevron's, built in 1902 and processing two hundred and forty-thousand barrels of crude a day—emit more than two million pounds of waste per year. The Environmental Protection Agency has recorded hundreds of spills, most of which run into adjacent neighborhoods. Groundwater has been contaminated by benzene, ethylbenzene, toluene, and xylenes, and soils by toxic heavy metals like chromium, lead, nickel, and vanadium. Locals complain that their children have chronic asthma, skin rashes, recurring nosebleeds, and coughing attacks. Throughout Contra Costa County, residents are exposed to sixty tons of benzene, thirty tons of formaldehyde, and smaller amounts of other carcinogens every year, all from six aging refineries: hence the name Cancer Belt, a region more responsible for emitting climate change gasses than any other in the state.

Richmond appears in the *Contra Costa Times* almost daily because of yet another shooting or stabbing. The poverty there is appalling despite the fact that Chevron, California's largest corporation, with its headquarters located comfortably in nearby San Ramon, circulates billions of dollars a year through Richmond while brazenly circumventing numerous environmental safety regulations. Its refinery has been cited for hundreds of accidents, including major fires, spills, leaks, explosions, toxic gas releases, flaring, and air contamination. A 1999 explosion caused by an old leaking valve shredded trees, took the fur off squirrels, and sent residents vomiting to the hospital. In 2007, a corroded pipe detonated in a blast heard twenty miles away. Yet nobody seems to be asking whether the human devastation in Richmond, whose children are hospitalized for asthma twice as often as anywhere else in the county, somehow parallels this ecological devastation. Meanwhile, as death rates from cardiovascular and respiratory diseases remain higher than the statewide levels, and as female reproductive cancers double the county's overall rate, Chevron pays its fines, controls the local Chamber of Commerce, employs relatively few locals, refuses to disclose how it disposes of its mercury, uses overseas shelters to avoid federal taxes, and fixes nothing. Much the same is true of Shell, whose refinery enshadows Martinez, and whose profits from dark liquids sucked from the underworld fund the Walnut Creek Lesher Center for the Arts and its peppy 1940s musicals.

The cul-de-sac insularity, the fabulous soil fecundity, the Ghost Fleet timelessness of old fighting ships in mothballs, the Avalonian alleys of nightmare and dream resonate together symbolically, with Contra Costa an Other World of green valleys and compromised playgrounds, cherry trees and shell casings, all of it held in the rocky gaze of cloud-wrapped Mt. Diablo. Places are more than aggregates of people and planning zones. Alive beyond the sum of their measurable parts, places exhibit a style of being, a geographic personality, even a spirit or soul whose social, ecological, historical, and architectural forms coalesce like the gestures, gaits, glances, and vocal mannerisms of familiar individuals. And just as tabulating gestures, gaits, glances, and mannerisms tells you little about the character of the person under scrutiny, so it is with the soul of place, better discerned by patient study, mythic imagination, and intuitive feel. Building a relationship that appreciates such localized uniqueness captures more flavors and colors and metaphors than any examination operated from inside a fantasy of objectivity.

When we disrupt the character of a place through conquest, pollution, or wanton destruction, that disruption too repeats itself symbolically in the stories gathered in that place. To abuse that ground is to abuse its soul and its stories. In other words, we give the place an *ecological complex* that persists until we do the hard relational work of repair, appreciation, and healing.

As I began reluctantly to think about the great mass of unvocalized California waiting out there beyond the mission counties I had surveyed, an unexpected wanderlust came over me. As an activity of soulseeing rather than sightseeing, terrapsychological exploration of the spirit or soul of places does not pay well—aside from an occasional book and lecture it does not pay at all; but by doing it we bring new meanings and responsibilities to the ancient role of cosmographer. They were right after all, those wandering transdisciplinarians, to draw their maps animated by mysterious, marauding, and often monstrous presences: "Beyond This Point, There Be Dragons."

TWO MILLION YEARS AGO, what would become mighty Mt. Diablo began to rise around a core of oceanic crust (ophiolite rocks), marine sediment, and igneous rock. Around this core wrapped a geologic Franciscan Complex (speaking of complexes) of far older greenstone, sandstone, and chert, with some schist, shale, coal, conglomerate, and limestone mixed in and layered. Today, shell fossils dot trails on the mountain and peek out of shoulders of stone: remnants of ocean flooring brought so high above California that the United States Regular Land Survey of 1851 aligned townships all over the southwest from these peaks raised up from the depths.

Bobcats, gray foxes, coyotes, black-tailed deer, feral pigs, raccoons, whipsnakes, rattlers, and even tarantulas live up here with peregrine falcons, black-chinned sparrows, and sharp-shinned hawks. Butterflies drift through stands of manzanita, black sage, black walnut, elderberry, Coulter pine, and many varieties of oak. A species of fairy lantern, also known as globe tulip, is endemic to this place.

So were the Volvon group of the Bay Miwok once. They lived at the southeastern base of the mountain for time out of mind before

Spanish missionaries came in the late 1700s to save them from their unshriven selves and their bowl-shaped homes of willow and grass. Most of the survivors were marched off to Mission San Jose to the south in what is now Alameda County.

Not everyone adapted to the barred enclosures of a religious regimen. When a group of native inmates escaped between 1803 and 1806, they eluded the force sent to capture them by vanishing into the bushes in what is now Buchanan Field in Concord. The Spaniards blamed their inability to recapture the escapees on the intervention of a devilish (*diablo*) spirit, and so by 1834, the land grant given to Salvio Pacheco was called Rancho Monte del Diablo. According to Mariano Vallejo, however, this incident actually took place at the foot of the mountain.

Who was this devil? The Volvon had no idea until they met him at the mission. The notion of a supreme evil being derived not from Testaments Old or New, but from early church ideology, when the legalists and literalists were busy making dominant their version of Christianity. This was the same group that demonized the Gnostics for following an inward path to God, laughing at literalist interpretations of Scripture, and allowing women to serve as clergy. Having claimed spiritual descent from Peter himself, the legalists were allies of the Emperor Constantine by the time he made Christianity the official religion of Rome in the fourth century.

"Pagan" Romans had called their morning star Lucifer ("Light-Bearer"). This is why the name does not appear as such in the Bible. Only later was it co-opted into the now-necessary idea of Satan: necessary psychologically and politically because of the growing collective need to project the institutionalized believer's darkest impulses beyond the institution. Even now, for example, the Roman Catholic Church blames its ongoing and systematic failure to protect young people abused by priests on Satan's attempts to undermine the Vatican's holy authority, not on a centuries-old culture of cover-up, minimization, denial, misdirection, and violence. Within the iron circle of this self-serving logic, catastrophe and failure are twisted into signs of success: why else would the Evil One redouble his efforts against the armies of God? Nevertheless, far above the madness, the morning star rises and shines.

The Volvon, who believed themselves created on this spot by Prairie Falcon Man and his grandfather, Coyote Man, were careful to live at the base of the mountain, ascending its grassy slopes only for sacred ceremonies at the top. It would not have surprised them that Mountain House, a hotel built on those slopes in 1874, burned down, or that a Hearst attempt to found a resort after that succumbed to bankruptcy. The Volvon told tales in which White-Footed Mouse stole fire from the people of the Central Valley to the east. (Trickster as a creator god who steals fire for humankind is a worldwide mythologem.) Carrying the fire in his magic flute, White-Footed Mouse climbed Mt. Diablo and set free such a blaze of warmth and illumination that people saw it for miles on every side. By 1928, a ten-million-candlepower beacon was turned on at the summit. John Muir had watched the sun come up from here in 1877 and called the sight "glorious."

All in all, Mt. Diablo made a good place to visit to obtain a higher view.

From the observation deck at the top I could see the undulating mists over the Livermore Valley to the south, the towers of the distant Golden Gate Bridge to the west, and the curve of the San Joaquin River to the north. Below me, folds of Diablo bore dark blotches, the scars wrought by mercury and coal mining.

Finally, I faced east and looked out over the Great Central Valley of California.

The Valley is the oldest part of California, the Coast Ranges and Sierras having risen on either side of it roughly 3.5 million years ago. Those stony formations contained the tuna-swum waters of an ancient inland sea until what is now the Sacramento River finally broke through into San Francisco Bay. The river runs south; the San Joaquin runs north to join it in a watery pairing of opposites at the Delta.

As the Valley emptied, it turned into an enormous swamp collecting rich alluvial soils running down from the mountains to coat its very flat sea-level expanse. Of the world's ten basic soil types, nine reside there on a floor of sandy loam sealed from below by mineralized clay that farmers know as hardpan. The climate—hot in spring and summer with little rain—is like that of Egypt. Without irrigation and nitrogen, agribusiness worth $36 billion a year could not sell fruits and vegetables tugged season after season from the weary ground.

I shook my head and rubbed a stiffness from the small of my back near where my rump had rested too long against a car seat. I had been through so much on my terrapsychological hellrides through coastal California that an end to further fieldwork had come to seem like a blessing. Besides, that's what graduate students were for. Especially the younger ones craving the shocks and perils of initiation into the psychic reality of place. *Tears* was named *Tears* for good reason.

Yet as I stared across the valley toward the distant Sierras, an uncanny mood filtered through me. With my thoughts coming to a halt, my heart seemed to melt into a dark, electric fluid that began to circulate throughout my body. My fingertips and toes began to tingle. What lore, what mysteries, what strange reenactments, buried histories, and treasures of symbol and myth cooked and pulsed within the great inland belly of my homeland? *Beyond This Point, There Be Dragons...*

Although my face felt stiff from the chilly wind, I knew I had begun to smile even before seeing it reflected in a window pane: a glimpse of a recalled terrapsychologist trudging down the ancient mountain. My camera and notebook were waiting for me in the waterproof shoulder bag formerly carried up and down El Camino Real between San Diego and Sonoma. I still did not know why Aphrodite's lovely, angry image had scolded me in a dream. But I understood that, come what may, some of us living between the empyrean and the plankton just have to know what's over that next horizon.

MT. DIABLO, CONTRA COSTA COUNTY, and Hercules: three of many, perhaps countless, examples of how ecological complexes tend to express themselves in the language of myth.

As the scrupulous work of C.G. Jung, James Hillman, Joseph Campbell, Hermann Hesse, Thomas Mann, Christine Downing, Marija Gimbutas, Ginette Paris, Karl Kerenyi, Rudolf Otto, Mircea Eliade, James Frazer, and a host of modern and ancient mythographers has amply demonstrated, myth has ever served as a language for delineating deeply felt connections between the human and the nonhuman. Aphrodite as a figure in story, painting, or dream images erotic ties whose attractions bind up the cosmos, from the quantum foam recalling her birth near the seashore to the pull and dance of distant galaxies. Even the word "cosmos" comes from a Greek term referring to adornments and cosmetics such as those favored by the goddess of love and beauty.

Like her sisters in other pantheons (e.g., Venus, Lakshmi, Enya, Branwen, Dierdre, Freya, Ishtar, Cliodhna), Aphrodite offers us a name and a presence for a specific pattern of relationships that enliven human spheres of knowing even while transcending them. Likewise, dieties such as Zeus, Jupiter, Odin, Ammon, Indra, and Dagda are more than characters in old tales: they personify the power of an elevated view, with "patriarchy" a vulgar literalization of what they potentially stand for. Athena, Minerva, Inanna, Durga, Sekhmet, Fatimah, Belisama, Brigid, Saraswati, and White Buffalo Calf Woman show us the feminine face of archetypal Wisdom. Dionysus, Bacchus, Osiris, Orpheus, Shiva, Sarapis, Dumuzi, Izanagi, and Krishna perform the redemptive possibilities in states dramatic and ecstatic, and Demeter, Sita, Isis, Gefion, Cerridwen, and Ceres feed us hints of the nourishing bounty of nature, with Freyr and Saturn patiently tending the harvest.

All these beings of myth join us to the more-than-human world by lending imaginal forms to its intelligence and aliveness. Far from dead or irrelevant, myths spontaneously reinvent themselves wherever the gap between what we think and where we live widens into dissociation and breakdown. It's not a matter of myth versus reality, but of how conscious we can be of mythic reality.

For the ancients and the indigenous, each place held its own mythic presence, its own familiar, power, or *genius loci:* its distinctive spirit or soul. It's as though landscapes served as geographic altars.

Perhaps they still do.

Here in Contra Costa County, Pleasant Hill seems to be a playground for Psyche and Eros, with its name a reminder of their offspring Voluptas (Pleasure). The Greek figure Psi repeats itself in the birdlike wings of the streets that surround John F. Kennedy University. Having fought off absorption by Walnut Creek in 1961, the new city council of Pleasant Hill received a symbolic gift of bibs and baby bottles from mayors around the county. The romance of parents Psyche and Eros seasoned local author Alice Hobart's novel *The Cup and the Sword*, and the first play to air in the dome-shaped CineArts Theater: *Doctor Zhivago*. Psyche's famous lamp came up for discussion in 1959 when Walnut Creek promised to look after Pleasant Hill's street lighting, and again in the 1960s when the Architectural Review Committee limited the amount of neon signage in the newborn city. (While here, Hobart also penned *Oil for the Lamps of China*.) The tower that talked Psyche out of leaping to her death recurred in the water towers and windmills Pleasant Hill was once known for. Streets between Gregory and Taylor bear women's names: Psyche's sisters? The original land grant was Las Juntas, a feminine noun for "confluences"; Interstate 680 divides Pleasant Hill like Psyche's knife. One street is even named Cleaveland. Malls on and near Contra Costa Boulevard stand in for temples of Venus, a goddess not only of love but of possessions. Psyche, whose name also means "Soul," did time in such temples to remember herself before she lost herself.

Even before I un-retired and prepared for the Great Central Valley, I had begun to suspect from my reading about the place that it functioned as a kind of vast alchemical vessel, a mythic cauldron whose contents underwent slow but steady transformation. Heat, fermentation, high-pressure distillation, unending labor, technical innovation, and transformation of metals pulled from dark depths were all associated with the alchemical *Opus* or Great Work of artificers who strove for centuries to produce refined substances for healing, wisdom, and immortality. All those metaphors cooked and simmered in the objective reality of the Central Valley. I was not surprised to learn that the Valley contained even thicker blends of ethnic culture than Los Angeles (witness Fresno), or that so many who grew up in the giant vessel could not find the means to escape its invisible walls. The alchemists had called their labor with plants *spagyrics* ("spah-GEER-iks"), meaning to pull apart and put back together; Central Valley farmers called it agriculture as they pulled up and boxed the fruits of sweaty labor. "Our gold is not the ordinary gold," proclaimed the ancient adepts as they mixed their metals in a search for spirit hidden in matter; but plenty of ordinary gold awaited the miners who founded Sacramento with the merchants, bankers, barkeeps, and ministers who preyed on them. Some of the miners who worked dry ground called themselves "puffers," unconsciously adopting the derogatory term leveled by devoted alchemists at small-souled colleagues bent on snatching material wealth.

When you form such an idea about the style or character of a place, it raises the question of how much of what you sense is actually you instead of the place. Can landscapes be alive enough to suffer from complexes? Is the world beneath and around us truly alive and reactive, perhaps even speaking in a chthonic tongue we no longer understand? Or do we merely wish it so?

In terraspsycholoical work I have seen people misunderstand, project into, and fail to grasp the soul of their surroundings. I have done these things myself. When that happens, the contact goes dead. It's a discernible failure of relationship, as between human beings mired in miscommunication, that does not *create* a sense of animation in the land, but *smothers* it. Once this happens, the place is apt to reappear at night as a distressed dream character fighting to reestablish authentic contact. As investigators of the soul of place, we are also helped by feedback from people both inside and outside the field of activity, people who know us well enough to know when we deceive ourselves. They can also remind us that intuitions, associations, guesses, and flights of fancy need substantiating.

However, substantiation is not proof. The demand for proof is an artifact of the paradigm of modernity, or the "Big Machine" as I imagine this collective way of constructing reality. In other words, the demand for proof is generated by the same machinelike standards that regard the land as dead, a mere backdrop to human affairs, and the non-measurable as unreal. Mechanical thinking has reached so deeply into our psyches from the blinking gray equipment stacked around us that we have absorbed its characteristics: linearity, literal-mindedness, push-pull causality. Machines depend upon the tangible, the graspable. For them, what lives outside numbers, procedures, and programs cannot exist. Native Californian poet Shaunna Oteka McCovey puts it well in verse:

> **If you cannot see**
> *Istilleat*
> **between the lines**
> *allofmymeals*
> **then your collected facts**
> *witha*
> **will never constitute**
> *musselshell*
> **knowledge.**

Categorically denying that the land calls out to us deeply enough to infiltrate our moods and dreams, symptoms and settlements (are they actually unsettlements?) implies that self and Earth, inscape and landscape are separate entities. To an analytical, machine-like eye blind to the encompassing medium of water, one fish swerving as another swam by it would wrongly suggest that the first had been acted upon directly by a force emanating from the second. We would not try prove that the right hand causes the left because we know this would pose the wrong question; yet we forget that empiricism, literalism, and quantification, although useful for studying controlled events, offer no substitute for the hard labor of forming more complicated relationships. The family farmer who loves his crops and soils knows them more intimately through his hands and heart, as well as his mind, than the landlord who profits from what he thinks of only as productive real estate.

What would we perceive differently, and with more than our relation-pulverizing intellect involved, if we looked at geographical features as psychical qualities, and at places where we live or work as repositories of powerful tales joining us to the lands we occupy?

I drove out into the Central Valley in recollection of those cosmographers who learned whatever they could about the places they visited, their colorfully painted and labeled maps drawn to describe and evoke rather than to predict or control. If my alchemical fantasy took me nowhere, I could always junk it and find a more useful one along the way. If nothing else, these sojourns would open a chance to breach the Coast Ranges and come finally to terms with the mysterious interiority of "the other California."

Introduction:
"It's California."

Ruthie and Winfield scrambled down from the car,
and then they stood, silent and awestruck, embar-
rassed before the great valley. The distance was
thinned with haze, and the land grew softer and
softer in the distance. A windmill flashed in the
sun, and its turning blades were like a little helio-
graph, far away. Ruthie and Winfield looked at it,
and Ruthie whispered, "It's California."

– John Steinbeck, *The Grapes of Wrath*

It was eventually called Pangaea, the supercontinent, but it began to
fall apart about a hundred and seventy-five million years ago.

The Jurassic Era dinosaurs of that time probably didn't notice—
the breakup was too slow to be noticeable to mortal eyes—but as

15

North America drifted away from what would become Africa, Europe, and South America, the tectonic mass of the Farallon Plate began grinding its way beneath North American near its west coast, where Utah is today. The grinding built the southern Rocky Mountains.

As the Farallon continued to move eastward, it pulled islands and chunks of sea floor with it, leaving them to collide in the future Utah, piling on in terrane accretions that moved the coastline farther and farther west. Eventually they were joined by what had been part of the Pacific sea floor. Later still, mountain ranges rose to the west and east of this flooring: the future Central Valley of California, flatter every century as sediment from either side washed down into it over five million years and solidified in hard layers of Mesozoic shale and sandstone. Melting snow from the Sierras ran into the Valley, turning it into the vast inland sea mentioned in Native Californian legends that were ancient before cities rose in Mesopotamia.

When this inland sea found its way to the Pacific via San Francisco Bay, the Valley drained, leaving gray soils of granitic alluvium on its east side and brown sedimentary alluvium on its west side. With the Cascades to the north, Sierras to the east, Coast Ranges to the west, and the Temblors, Tehachapis, and Sierras plugging the southern end like a stopper, the Valley found itself insulated, its flat floor sealed by hardpan. Within this great Valley, two other valleys lay end to end: the Sacramento to the north, drained by its river, and the San Joaquin, the southern counterpart, also drained by a river. The two rivers met at the Sacramento-San Joaquin Delta, a wetland of tules and rich peat soil.

For a time, more than a million acres of freshwater marshland, valley grassland, and fog-soaked riparian woodland spread through the Valley. Having become the first Europeans to enter, making their way among lupines and clovers, Spanish soldiers deserting their post in San Diego in the late 1700s would have seen rivers packed with salmon and steelhead trout; ducks, geese, antelope, elk, deer, grizzly bears, wolves, and condors; and so many geese that later hunters would hit them just by pointing their blazing shotguns upward.

In pre-conquest days three centuries ago, a hundred and sixty thousand Natives in three hundred tribelets lived in the Valley: Maidu and Wintun in the north, Yokuts in the south, Miwoks in between. Although most spoke a version of the Penutian language family, their dialects and customs were nearly as diverse as the lush biodiversity of the plants and animals among which they moved with millennia of well-researched confidence.

On the coast, Spanish missionaries landed in 1769. Their goal was to secure Alta California for the Spanish crown, converting the Indians to serve as soldiers and laborers. The primary tool to achieve this was a Mission system developed during the Spanish Reconquista that drove the Moors out of Iberia. Forces under Ferdinand and Isabella had built missions to incarcerate and con-vert their captured enemies. Padre Presidente and Inquisitor Junípero Serra transplanted this system to California. Serra had tried this in Baja, but by the time his men left, most of the native inhabitants were dead or dying of syphilis and smallpox. He remained undeterred.

In 1772, Father Juan Crespí and Captain Pedro Fages left the mission outpost in San Diego and made their way northward to explore the land and seek suitable locations for missions. Making their way over the spur of Mt. Diablo, they camped near Antioch at the western edge of the Central Valley where the San Joaquin and Sacramento Rivers meet. Crespí wrote,

> We ascended a pass to its highest point in order to make observations, and we saw that the land opened into a great plain as level as the palm of the hand, the valley opening about half the quadrant, sixteen quarters from northwest to southeast, all level land as far as the eye could reach.

Finding their trek blocked by the San Joaquin River, they detoured south to Monterey.

That year Father Francisco Garces came with a telescope, quad-rant, and diary to scout the San Joaquin Valley. He also carried a small canvas with the Virgin Mary painted on one side and the Devil in Hell on the other. This dualistic diagram was for converting the local Indians, most of whom were not interested. Nevertheless, the Yokuts greeted Garces with friendship and feasting; he performed the first Valley baptism near Delano, a Yokuts village, in 1776. In 1781, he was killed during an uprising of the Yuma Indians.

1805 brought Lieutenant Gabriel Moraga from Mission San Jose. He too was scouting the Valley for mission sites. None were built there, but he named the Kings River draining from the Sierras into vanished Tulare Lake after the three fabled wise men who followed their star, the San Joaquin after his father (who was named after the father of Mary), the Mariposa ("butterfly"), and the Merced for its mercy toward his hot, thirsty men. All in all he made forty-six trips into the Valley, but the Yokuts held out, raiding guns, ammunition, and horses from the mission forces sent to round up recruits. Their intra-valley communications and intelligence network usually kept them apprised of troop movements, although James Savage, a former soldier with several Indian wives, managed to kill twenty natives near Fresno Dome and scatter the Ahwahneechees in Yosemite. Later, ill and hungry Maidu forced to march from Camp Bidwell in Chico to Round Valley in the 1850s perished by the hundreds.

John C. Fremont had been traveling through California and Oregon in the 1840s making maps, writing to his sixteen-year-old wife, and looking forward to the Mexican-American War. His instigations of insurrection among American settlers recently arrived in California would culminate in the brief Bear Flag Revolt shortly before the annexation of California by the U.S. in 1848. Having survived much hardship, including hunger (he ate his dog Tiamat just before the Sierra supply train arrived), he bought and carved out Rancho Las Mariposas in 1857 and became the San Joaquin Valley's first cattle baron.

Jose Noriega had set up a cattle ranch near Brentwood in 1836. From him John Marsh bought land at the foot of Mt. Diablo the following year after traveling overland across the continent. He was known primarily for the high prices he charged his medical patients (although he did not have a medical license) and visitors who bought supplies at his Rancho Los Meganos ("sand dunes"). "He is perhaps the meanest man in California," pioneer John Bidwell wrote. In letters Marsh referred to native children as "easily domesticated," especially with corporal punishment. Seeing skeletal remains near what is now Stockton, he named the place Calaveras ("skulls"). On his way to Martinez in 1856, Marsh was murdered by three employees angry about the low wages he doled out to them.

In 1848 John Audubon came through and saw a herd of at least a thousand elk. In 1860 geologists Josiah Dwight Whitney and William Brewer led the first state survey. John Muir entered the Valley in the spring nine years later and waded through a shallow sea of lupines, mints, blackberries, gilias, corollas, and many wildflowers he could not name. "Oftentimes on awakening," wrote Muir, who felt he'd been walking through liquid gold, "I would find several new species learning over me and looking me full in the face, so that my studies would begin before rising."

Coastal California was colonized and industrialized by missions and then rails, but the Central Valley mainly by rails. The first line had connected Sacramento with Folsom in 1856; within four years the Southern Pacific began engineering a railroad the length of the Valley, controlling eleven and a half million acres and installing in Roseville the largest railroad assembly yard west of the Mississippi. Towns sprang up around train depots and packing factories.

By that time farmers in the Valley were growing grains, adding fruits and vegetables in the 1870s with the invention of the refrigerated train car. The railroads brought the Chinese, and trains connected towns founded or settled by former Southern Confederates looking for new places to plant crops. Around them, the Californio owners, devastated by cattle losses to floods and drought, were losing vast estates to incoming Americans whose courts made easy work of invalidating the owners' *diseños* (informal property maps). By contrast, maps drawn by Fremont's cartographer Charles Preuss proved highly influential in propagandizing the American conquest of California.

With help from the courts and the Federal Government, the enormous ranchos of the Californios transmuted easily into gigantic American agricultural operations. Arriving as a naval officer in 1846, Edward F. Beale consolidated four Mexican land grants into

Rancho Tejon in southern Kern County. By the 1870s, when German immigrants Henry Miller and Charles Lux ran the largest cattle business in the West (and the Main Canal to irrigate it), half of California was owned by .2% of its population.

All through the coming century, vast tracts of land—now irrigated by a Central Valley Project (CPV) drawing water southward from Shasta Dam—came under ever more consolidated corporate control as the Valley's agricultural potential built toward and passed $20 billion a year.

The Great Central Valley of California: today, four hundred and thirty miles long and seventy-five miles at its widest. Looking from the air like a patchwork of flat, linear shapes, it reaches across forty-two thousand square miles of fifteen million mostly industrialized acres from Kern County to Tehama County, from Fort Tejon to Redding. The Valley produces a quarter of the table food bought and sold in the U.S., including 100% of the nation's raisins, 90% of plums, 60% of table grapes and almonds, 40% of peaches, safflowers, cantaloupes, and potatoes, 30% of walnuts, 20% of carrots and tomatoes, 20% of cotton, and nearly all the nation's artichokes, apricots, avocados, nectarines, prunes, melons, tomatoes, and peaches. Rice under cultivation occupies five hundred thousand acres.

To mass produce food in an alchemical oven the size of England requires a titanic mechanized infrastructure. The Valley holds more than fourteen hundred dams and thousands of miles of levees, canals, and aqueducts; the CVP pumps seven million acre-feet of water a year toward Bakersfield. Four hundred thousand acres of watersheds are logged every year, increasing runoff, erosion, and sedimentation. Cattle graze over seventy-thousand square miles a year: in all, more than half the total watershed area of the state.

As soil disappears under advancing urban sprawl, what's left—two thirds of California's tillable farmland—suffers from extreme chemical dependency, with four tons of pesticides per square mile dumped on the crops every year. As nitrate fertilizers exhaust the soils, ammonium emissions mix with smog to hang health hazards over entire cities. By 2001, the EPA designated the San Joaquin Valley a severely polluted ozone region. Cherrie Moraga sums it up:

> The hundreds of miles of soil that surround the
> lives of Valley dwellers should not be confused
> with land. What was once land has become dirt,
> overworked dirt, overirrigated dirt, injected with
> deadly doses of chemicals and violated by every
> manner of ground- and back-breaking machinery.
> The people that worked the dirt do not call what
> was once the land their enemy. They remember
> what land used to be and await its second coming.

The ecological costs are enormous and rising. Aquifers near
depletion, with the San Joaquin Valley alone pumping 1.3 million
acre-feet of groundwater a year beyond what's replenishable. Total
water use in the Sacramento River Basin crests at eighteen billion
cubic meters per year. Only 4% of the Central Valley's original
wildlife remains, and only 1% of its original woodlands. As bur
clover, ripgut, foxtails, wild oats, and Johnsongrass spread like the
weeds they are, native perennial bunch grasses, three-awn, and nee-
dle grass rapidly disappear.

> From the air, the valley revealed itself most fully for
> what it truly was: an imposition of will—of pattern
> and abstract organization—on endless stretches of
> resistant, heat-hardened clay. Across a century,
> great public works, ferocious machines, and the
> back-breaking labor of millions now forgotten had
> brought into being a place that nature never
> intended, a place, like so much of California, pos-
> sessed of an instability, a fault line, just beneath the
> tranquilly patterned landscape.
>
> – Kevin Starr, *Coast of Dreams*

A landscape owned by corporations rather than by its occupants. By the late twentieth century, the Times Mirror-controlled

Tejon Ranch stood at two hundred seventy thousand acres, the sixth largest privately owned property in the U.S. Run by descendants of Henry Miller, the Bowles Farming Company owned fourteen thousand acres in Merced County and extensive riparian rights along the San Joaquin River. Another descendant, Nickel Enterprises, held eight thousand acres in Kern, Fresno, and Merced Counties. In Modesto, Gallo controls seventeen thousand acres (as well as a third of all the wine and brandy business in the U.S.). Boswell owns a hundred and forty thousand acres. All told, more than 70% of the San Joaquin and Sacramento Valleys remain privately owned.

Relatively little revenue from these large operations comes back into the Valley. In the San Joaquin, 26% of children live below the poverty line, education is faltering, as are basic health services, and teen pregnancy rates are going out of sight. With the recession of 2008, some Valley towns staggered under unemployment rates above 50%. Furthermore, studies show that urban and suburban sprawl results not only in pollution, smog, and crime, but weakened public services, lower quality of life, fewer investment and job opportunities, and bond debt; Fresno, debt free in 1980s, carried $329 million in bond debt for infrastructure by 1999. Through the 1990s, more Anglo families in California received financial aid, food stamps, and other public assistance than any other ethnic group, especially in the Central Valley. As farmland vanishes and smog increases enough to cut into production, food prices only escalate.

Extremes of poverty and wealth have sharply stratified Valley culture. Few are surprised when children do not graduate from school, let alone fail to attend college. A legacy of equating upward mobility with selling one's soul leaves an abiding sense of discontented fatalism here, especially in low-income families. Dust and mist frequently erase the horizon, but so can lack of opportunity. The nickname "Prison Valley" refers to the "gray gold" of penitentiaries in Madera, Corcoran, Delano, Avenal, Wasco, Chino, Folsom, Ione, Soledad, Stockton, Tracy, and Vacaville.

Yet the Valley retains its alchemical capacity for profound transformation. The diversity of perspectives, skills, cultures, religions, and ethnicities (a "laboratory of races" says Anne Loftis) fully matches the diversity of crops. After the Californios, Americans, and Chinese came the Sikhs, African Americans, Armenians, Mexicans, Japanese, Vietnamese, Laotians, Cambodians, and more than a hundred other ethnic groups. During the 1930s, arrivals included people from Minnesota, Arizona, Mississippi, Utah, New Mexico, Oregon, Washington, Colorado, the Dakotas, Nebraska, Kansas, Missouri, Texas, Arkansas, and Oklahoma, those last four states contributing three hundred and fifty thousand newcomers here to farm, ranch, or drill for oil. Half the Hmong settled in the U.S. after the fall of Saigon, many in California. By 2000, the Valley's minorities had become its majority. Along with churches sprouted mosques, temples, and shrines.

> The real problem is that too many people—including some who claim to be experts—don't recognize that California is a collection of distinct regions, of unique histories and experiences, of varied people gathered under one name. It has no single homogenous core—unless it is hope.
>
> – Gerald Haslam, *The Other California*

Here was a California almost wholly unfamiliar to me, raised as I had been on the coast. Like many Californians I had passed through here rapidly, stopping only long enough along Interstates 5 or 99 for burgers or gasoline. Now I was here to listen, feel, and learn, place by place and county by county.

I brought questions with me. How would such a long, flat, parceled-up and industrialized landscape affect its inhabitants psychologically? How did it translate into the stuff of interiority: landscape into mindscape and soulscape? What were its guiding images and metaphors? What could be dreamed out here? What did the Valley spend its days and nights alchemizing?

> Unlike the mountains or the coast, the valley is a "forgiving" landscape whose subtle textures of oak

drape and tule mound, cottonwood glitter and willow blur, stroke the heart and evoke tenderness. At
their best, Central Valley land and waterscapes are
nature at its most eloquent: hieroglyph, thicket of
the imagination and psyche.

– Richard Meisinger

The alchemists of old insisted that the *prima materia*, the "prime
matter" to be worked into an agent of transformation, was found
not in temples or on mountaintops but in low places. I decided,
therefore, to start at the bottom of the Valley, as yet unaware that
what I saw there would change me forever.

Part One:
San Joaquin Valley
(Blackening and Whitening)

Fort Tejon (*separatio*)

I began reading science fiction in sixth grade, when Arthur C. Clarke was one of my favorite authors. In his novel *Rendezvous with Rama* he describes vividly what it's like to stand inside the vast, metal belly of an alien machine so enormous that what seems like a plain curves away into sky.

Driving up the Grapevine and through the Tejon Pass into the Central Valley brought that image forcibly to mind. As shoulders of granite parted and fell away to either side of the highway, the Valley appeared before me, a flat, checkerboard plain of green and tan squares stretching far away out of view. I pulled off Interstate 5 for a longer look. The sheer immensity of it startled the eye and filled the heart with awe. I tried to imagine this vista before the highway or any but the humblest human structures.

Production. That word characterizes what the San Joaquin Valley, named after a frustrated father who prayed for penance in the desert, has come to mean to its most recent occupiers. Its more than twenty-seven thousand square miles arranged over eight counties produce hundreds of food crops, cotton, coal, natural gas, steam, oil, various mined metals, water for Southern California via the California Aqueduct, and energy from wind and sun. At its southern end, Kern County, named for a river named after a man it nearly drowned, is parched and mountainous. The sun shines an average of three hundred days a year here, with temperatures rising well over a hundred in the summer.

In 1853, Edward Beale, Superintendent of Indian Affairs, installed five military reservations in Oregon, Utah, and California. One of them, the Sebastian Indian Reservation, lay within Tejon ("badger") Ranch at the bottom of the Central Valley just northeast of Los Angeles. This ranch comprised four land grants: Ranchos la Liebre, el Tejon, los Alamos y Agua Calienta, and de Castaic, in all, two hundred thousand acres bought by Beale for $90,000 between 1866-67. He irrigated the place, supplied its fort, and ran cattle through the scrub-covered hills. Jefferson Davis helped him introduce camels into the U.S., but most of them ran away. (Beale had also been busy in Washington D.C., where a gold sample he brought began the Gold Rush.)

Fort Tejon's location was strategic. Troops from the fort guarded local ranchers against cattle rustlers and Mojave and Paiute Indian raiders and kept an eye on the relatively cooperative Emigdiano living nearby. Situated in Grapevine Canyon, the fort serves as the stopper or lowermost sphincter for the alchemical vessel of the Great Central Valley.

Most of the fort's buildings fell down in 1857, when the San Andreas Fault (which meets the Garlock Fault just north of the fort) suddenly split, an immense alchemical *separatio* worth 8.3 on the Richter Scale. Today a wooden bridge leads over a creek to the Fort Tejon State Historical Park and its handful of old buildings, historical markers, and rattlesnake warning signs.

I spent little time in the main building, having seen my fill of posters under glass describing the displacement of native peoples as "The Inevitable Destiny." A walk through damp weeds led me into a long building housing racks of replica swords, coats, and hats for the troops. As I, a child of military families, ran a finger down the edge of one of the swords, a docent dressed as a soldier was complaining in the other room about a rude visitor who had just left. In alchemy the sword of *separatio* divides up the prime matter for further refinement. Here it separated fault blocks, cultures, and regions, but as yet I did not know what the Valley had been brewing.

In researching *The Tears of Llorona*, I went from county to county and place to place asking myself: *Who lives here, imaginally speaking? Which mythological face expresses this place's blend of geography, ecology, history, and culture?*

Who was here, mythically, at empty Fort Tejon? Janus, perhaps: the Roman name given to the god of doorways, latches, portals, covered passageways, and divisions of time, especially past and future. His faces point in two directions. January is named after him. Where he gazes, old periods end and new ones begin. Much of the Central Valley's American history started here, in this cleft between the hills, as the days of the Californios wound down to a bitter end.

In ancient Rome, the Janus Geminus, a small, thick-walled shrine, stood at the north end of the Forum. Its double doors were opened in times of war, closed in all-too-brief periods of peace. According to legend, the shrine was built after Janus unleashed volcanic fire and quaking from below to punish Romulus, a founder of the city, for his hubris and martial ambition. Many of his men were killed in this structure-collapsing cataclysm.

Janus also did a good turn or two for Saturn, god of the harvest and of agriculture, but also of lead, limitation, constriction, depression, hierarchy, authority, and obligation. All of these awaited on the other side of this defile. Yet Saturn, called Cronus by the Greeks and Freyr by the Norse, and the Greater Malefic by astrologers, was also known to antiquity as the bringer of a Golden Age. The Hindu knew him as mighty, beneficent Rama. Which version of him awaited on the flat plain up ahead?

Very often a dream that visits just before an event brings a sense of what that event will mean. But dreams don't stay in the dream world. Was some as-yet unknown *separatio* in the offing? Present-day pop alchemists with borderline tendencies like to insist, Great Mother fashion, that everyone and everything belongs in the opus, one big happy chemical family of substances, but the ancient adepts who did the actual experimentation saw things differently. At the end of the work, the residuum left in the bottom of the vessel—the *terra damnata* or *caput mortuem*—had to be thrown out so it could not spoil the results.

Had I come here to get rid of something? To separate out or away from something no longer useful?

Over the years of exploring California terrapsychologically, listening in on each town, city, or county, I had watched much that was once precious drop away with each new thing I learned. My desire to do psychotherapy, my hope for settling somewhere green permanently, my wish to find one school at which to teach instead of almost a dozen.... friends, colleagues, lovers, family... Had I been called out here to oversee more losses? If so, would they tell me more about losses past and present recorded in the land around me? Would I want to know, and if so, how much more? When would it be time to stop?

With a land base nearly as large as Los Angeles, Tejon Ranch remains a large player in industrial and business park development, especially to the west of here. They also invest in resorts and what their literature refers to as "sustainable" housing projects. Could be; yet here where it started, empty buildings stand as a shrine in quiet remembrance of the consequences of reach exceeding grasp.

Outside again I looked up through the chilly autumn light to see oaks perched on the rounded shoulders of hills soon to be twilit. The sense of desolation slowly dissipated as I drove thirty-eight miles north to Bakersfield, having transitioned from 5 to 99.

Bakersfield (*nigredo*)

By wiping out cattle, the basis of Californio economy, the great floods of 1862-3 wiped out the Californios as well. The sunny days in which these ranchero settlers from Mexico and Spain patrolled vast estates on horseback came abruptly to an end. Their land grants, surpassing eight hundred in number, passed into the hands of American settlers.

The flooding also benefited Harvey Brown and Colonel Thomas Baker, who took advantage of it to buy four hundred thousand acres of swampy land on the road from Los Angeles to Stockton. When the land finally dried out in 1863, Baker bought out Harvey, and three years later he laid out a town. This proved easier than it might have due to Baker's background in surveying and land law. He would also lay out Visalia and throw a dam across Buena Vista Lake.

Like Faust before him, Baker first embarked on a project of reclamation. Relying on Indian labor, he cleared away underbrush, redug shallow, stagnant wells, and drained malarial swamps until Captain Elisha Stephens arrived to become the first settler of "Kern Island." Baker's dams and canals moved water around a flood control levee into the South Fork Canal, a well-engineered appropriation for which he received numerous complaints along with tracts of land. When the state took them back, he resorted to forming a new town site.

31

By 1868 Baker had opened a real estate office to sell plots of lands to settlers, but he died of pneumonia—drowned, one might say— four years later during a typhoid fever epidemic. The town was named in remembrance of "Baker's field," ten acres of alfalfa he grew near his home at 19th and N Street.

With the Southern Pacific planting rails in the Central Valley, the Chinese came to town and settled at 20th Street between K and L. More than a thousand African Americans arrived as laborers to work in the fields of Kentucky attorneys James Ben Al Haggin and Lloyd Tevis. The laborers grew and harvested cotton, just as they had in the Deep South. Haggin and Tevis would eventually collide with Lux and Miller in seventy-six lawsuits involving eighty-six canal companies. Already the Valley was being targeted by bare-knuckle opportunists of the type that would dominate it one day.

Something about Bakersfield resisted reclamation, however, in part because it had been placed in the occasional path of the Kern River rather than beside it. A fire in 1889 burned everything but Scribner's water tower. By the early 1900s, Bakersfield found itself wallowing in deep debt after trustees had spent recklessly to entice the Southern Pacific Railroad into the newly incorporated city, only to see the rails head for Sumner (later Kern, now East Bakersfield). Plumbing and irrigation ran through filthy ditches; dust lay in the streets; disease flourished in stagnant pools of outhouse runoff: all in all, a smelly study in alchemical *putrefactio*, a slow, fetid decomposition. The city disincorporated. Some said that the old homestead on Reeder's Hill, where Baker had looked around the first time at the reach of his hydraulic empire-to-be, was haunted by a man who shot himself on the porch; another hung himself by the rafters. A land agent named Herrington was tarred and feathered there.

About this time James and Jonathan Elwood struck oil on the property of Tom Means. Although Los Angeles oil tycoon and miner Edward Doheny would buy out Means, twelve thousand barrels a day were gushing in newly drilled Kern oil fields by 1901. Beneath the ground, oil began to commune with the once-pure waters of the Kern River.

This prosperity set off a swampy boom in Bakersfield, where events quickly took on the darkening aspects of a liquid

Underworld: naked miners covered with asphaltum like black Eldorados, some with missing fingers; roads paved by wood blocks dipped in the tarry residue; prostitutes hanging empty dresses on posts in the red light district... Photographs taken of Bakersfield and its surroundings at the time of the oil boom show ebon derricks, isolated barracks-like houses in rows, treeless roads over empty landscapes, bare soil churned into mud, and dark, unreflecting pools, all of it under skies filled by plumes of black smoke. What people could be found were dwarfed by gigantic lattices erected to suck thick crude from the torn ground. The Yokuts had used the stuff to fashion death masks.

Rush Maxwell Blodget came to Bakersfield in 1884 at the age of three and spent part of his childhood there:

> "Out West" was always somewhere else. We were not Out West—No! No! True, we had saloons and dance halls, bartenders and gamblers, bad men and cowboys, sawdust floors and cuspidors, painted women and beer, and dead men on the barroom floor. But there was no romance in such things for us. Franz Buckreus was a very busy corner, and the Potters' Field at the Union Avenue Cemetery was a popular place for the boys who were slow on the draw.

At Chester Avenue he and some boys came across something dropped by a hooker:

> Once we found a letter you had dropped and in an alley, furtively we examined it, thinking the correspondence of a "madam" would be spicy. But the writer told you the news of a convent school and said you were the best mother in the whole world, and it was signed, "Your loving daughter, Elsie."

Once the Kern River and Coalinga oil fields were developed, oil-men looked around for more and found sources near Maricopa, McKittrick, Taft, and Lost Hills. Machinery for drilling and pumping displaced sheepherders and ranchers.

Although much had changed in Bakersfield by the time I arrived, the smell of oil had not: heavy and inescapable, it hung in the air even after dark. When the sun came up I walked out of the hotel and saw what the night had concealed: acres upon acres of derricks, tanks, and pipelines losing themselves in the hazy distance. The sign of a nearby construction supply business proudly announced, "Moving the Earth Since 1952."

Stopping long enough to see the Bakersfield Central Park, with its dark pools of water among scattered boulders behind a black fence, I drove up Panorama Drive and, parking near the Green Lawn Mortuary, trudged across the street from the park so I could look northward toward Oil City, the Kern River, and the hills beyond.

Nothing I had heard or read prepared me for the vista now below me. Wherever my eyes went, up, down, or sideways, they saw oil derricks and pipelines, a mechanical maze that covered the expanse all the way out to the horizon. I could not even begin to count the rigs, drills, tanks, and other installations, many in clanking, steaming, repetitive motion. The very landscape had been converted into one gigantic oil factory for as far as my gaze could reach.

When hard-faced men of industry brought petroleum to the surface and set it on fire for profit, they unwittingly unleashed the dark, lethal rivers of the Underworld. Wherever the poisonous ooze has been piped, corruption, violence, and death soon followed.

Underworld language permeates the industry. "Petroleum" literally means "rock oil," mined in 1870 by the first rich Rockefeller, who relied on intimidation, blackmail, fraud, and violence to dominate his competitors. Rockefeller: a hidden, skeletal, shadowy figure reminiscent of pale Pluto ("wealth"). "It is futile to resist," he is said to have warned his rivals. "Gasoline" goes back to *khaos* and "crude" to the Latin *crudus*: "rough," "raw," and "bloody." "Carbon" has a number of dark referents: "black," "burnt," "singe," "fire," "coal," "brazier," and "smoke." "Derrick" means "gallows" and "hangman."

Not long after Rockefeller began assembling Standard Oil, the first of the world-capturing multinational corporations, the first of thirteen petroleum disasters ignited Cleveland's Cuyahoga River into resemblance with Phlegethon, the burning river of Tartarus.

By the 1880s, the Standard Oil Trust controlled 90% of all refining in the U.S., 80% of all the nation's oil products, and 25% of total national crude output. The Sherman Antitrust Act eventually broke up the company on paper, but like the Hydra, it quickly spawned more heads. Today two are known as Chevron and ExxonMobil.

Big Oil money funded McKinley's Spanish-American War in 1898. It stood behind Harding, Coolidge, Calvin, and most of the U.S. Presidents after them, including Nixon, who was propped up by Gulf. Big Oil fought Franklin Delano Roosevelt's New Deal and scuttled his call for international regulation of the petroleum industry. Under John Archibald, Esso (the predecessor of ExxonMobil) provided the Spanish dictator Franco with free oil. FDR's embargo against Japanese oil supplies prompted them to attack Pearl Harbor so they could refuel in Indonesia. Texaco handed the Nazis a detailed assessment of the American aircraft industry. When Henri Deterding of Shell died, Hitler and Göring sent wreaths to his funeral. (Henry Ford also earned a Nazi medal, as did James Mooney of General Motors for providing trucks for the Nazi Blitzkrieg though France. GM would be instrumental in replacing the safe trolley transportation of the 1920s, when nine of ten trips were made by public transit, with buses and cars throughout the U.S., including in Fresno and Stockton.)

Britain and France carved up Iraq for oil in 1916 and threatened Iran, moves that earned the long-standing enmity of the Arab world. The CIA coup in Iran in 1953 to gain access to its oil ricocheted so badly that a reactionary government took the reins of power with relative ease. Exxon's 1960 decision to unilaterally cut Middle East oil prices led directly to the formation of OPEC.

Big Oil politicians had worked against regulation since the days of the original Standard Oil. Under the Reagan administration, deregulation and dropped antitrust suits led to vast increases in petroleum company mergers. As Reagan, George H.W. Bush, and

James Baker got busy making friends with Saddam Hussein, the introduction of the oil futures market further virtualized and destabilized a world economy now completely dominated by multinational companies subsidized, in the case of Big Oil, by the U.S. Government to the tune of billions a year.

No sooner did the cowboy boots of the second Bush administration stride into the White House than Dick Cheney sat down in private with an Energy Task Force convened to discuss the invasion of Iraq and the takeover of its petroleum supplies. The World Trade Center attack on September 11, 2001 accelerated plans already drawn. Soon soldiers' outposts in Iraq bore nicknames like Camp Exxon and Camp Shell. Because of U.S. dependency on Arabian oil, the fact that the 9/11 attackers were Saudis was downplayed in subsequent news reports, as was the fact that keeping U.S. troops in Arabia after the first Gulf War prompted Osama bin Laden to action. (U.S. visas used by the Saudi hijackers carried special privileges to facilitate the trade of oil.) Neither was much made of the connection between the ongoing war in Afghanistan begun after 9/11 and that country's strategic access to Caspian Sea fossil fuel sources.

Since 1999, Exxon had merged with Mobil, Chevron with Texaco, Conoco with Phillips, and British Petroleum (BP) with Amoco and then Arco to form the largest corporations the world has yet seen. In 2007, according to *Fortune*, the ten largest global oil companies made $167 billion in profits in 2006 alone. As of 2008, ExxonMobil, Chevron, ConocoPhillips, BP, Shell, and Valero controlled nearly 60% of the U.S. refining market, which was twice what they controlled twelve years before. They also controlled 60% of the nation's gas stations.

Today oilmen are bound together by a world-wrapping network of communications networks, banks, accountants, investment houses, directorships, and oil foundations. Oil money rivals some national economies, constructs fleets of tankers and lavish cities in the desert, lays down miles of tankage and pipes, pays for professional security armies. Oil revenues buy plastics, fertilizers, coal, drugs, alternative energy, and fully half the world's trade. Even the buildings in which oil companies reside are gigantic: the Gulf head-quarters in Pittsburgh, its heights topped by a pyramid; Mobil's tower in San Francisco; Texaco and Mobil facing off in New York City; BP in London with its own plaza, like the Chevron headquarters in San Ramon, California. The Petroleum Building in Houston, former headquarters to Texaco, once openly flew a skull-and-crossbones flag.

Most oil company profits come from trading, not from selling gasoline. Much of the world's refined oil sits in storage tanks, the transactions that maintain it defended as "proprietary." To take one example of where this leads: in 2006 ExxonMobil became the most profitable corporation in history, earning $39.5 billion in profits in a single year. The company made over $40 billion in profit in 2007, which was two-thirds more than Wal-Mart earned. ExxonMobil also spends generously—on more than forty front companies and supposed citizens' groups formed to make global warming evidence seem controversial; on lobbying for further deregulation of highly destabilizing energy futures trading, with $80 million spent on this from 1998 to 2006 (the top oil companies together spent $240 million); and of course on presidential and congressional elections.

All the big oil companies are major campaign spenders, with roughly 70% going to Republicans and the rest to Democrats to keep both parties in line. Big Oil gave record campaign money to the George W. Bush campaigns: $34 million for 2000 alone. It was money well spent. Bush named thirty former energy industry executives, lobbyists, and lawyers to influential posts in his administration; meanwhile, oil companies got Iraq and access to new national lands for drilling, $14 billion in tax breaks and new subsidies (some would consider this flagrant state socialism), and an easing of environmental regulations and controls. Washington's biggest lobby, the petroleum-supporting Chamber of Commerce, spent $338 million in federal lobbying from 1998-2008 and also lobbies ferociously against climate change legislation. Morgan Stanley and Goldman Sachs are also heavily involved in oil, so much so that they founded their own unregulated crude futures exchange. Many of the speculators are former employees of Enron.

Big Oil control remains firm at the state level too. For example, California sits on 3.5 billion barrels of its own petroleum, the nation's largest reserves in the ground. The state pumps six hundred and twelve thousand barrels a day, which comes to $27 million a day in oil company revenues. Proposition 87 (2006) would have introduced a severance tax on California oil like that of almost every other state. But Big Oil, including ExxonMobil and Chevron, defeated the proposition by convincing voters through front groups that gasoline prices would go up even higher. In the Golden State the top four refiners own 80% of the retail outlets and sell 90% of the gasoline, which is why gasoline prices in California are often the highest in the nation. There is no online resource for letting Californians know how to buy gasoline from an independent oil company.

Although the amount of oil pouring into U.S. markets has increased, gasoline availability has declined as gas stations and refineries close, demand rises, and oil companies maintain lower gasoline inventories on purpose. Accidents and spills at aging refineries multiply. Cars on American roads have doubled over the past few decades, but gas stations have declined by a third.

Nor are the real costs of oil production borne by the industries responsible. In 1996, for example, road congestion cost America's top seventy cities $74 billion for 4.6 million lost hours and 6.7 billion wasted gallons of fuel. Over the past twenty years, the world has seen thirty oil spills larger than the *Exxon Valdez*. Daily gasoline runoff from streets and driveways soaks eleven million gallons— one *Exxon Valdez* spill—into American waterways every eight months according to the National Academy of Sciences. The oil and gas industry generates more solid and liquid waste than all other municipal, agricultural, mining, and industrial sources combined.

Other minimum cost estimates for petroleum-driven air pollution in the U.S. alone include $54.7 billion in healthcare costs, $3-6 billion in reduced crop yields, $1-8 billion in building damage, $1.5 billion in water pollution, and untold ecological costs. (Every gallon of gasoline spews twenty-four pounds of heat-trapping emissions into the air.) Total annual costs to U.S. consumers of oil and auto industry subsidies and externalities comes to at least $128.5 billion a year. Independence Hall in Philadelphia, statues and tablets at Gettysburg, the Statue of Liberty, the Washington Monument, and other monuments to a nation's history melt in acid rain.

Health costs remain incalculable. Ninety million Americans live within thirty miles of an oil refinery. These refineries emit millions of pounds of benzene, butadiene, formaldehyde, nickel, lead, sulfur dioxide, nitrogen oxides, and other lethal pollutants. Oil refineries pumped over two hundred and fifty million tons of carbon dioxide into the air in 2004 alone and constitute the second greatest stationary source of greenhouse gases on Earth. (The first is the U.S. military.) They are the largest stationary U.S. source of volatile organic compounds (VOCs): air pollutants that include carcinogens and reproductive toxins that cause leukemia, lymphatic tissue cancers, birth defects, bronchitis, and emphysema. One of the worst, benzene, is a carcinogen dangerous at low levels and easily absorbed by breathing, ingestion, or skin contact. Nearly one in three Americans lives within thirty miles of an oil refinery like the three now operating in Bakersfield: according to the EPA, within the range of exposure to benzene concentrations in excess of the Clean Air Act's acceptable risk threshold.

Instead of cleaning up, oil profits fight new regulation, undermine current regulatory laws, thwart alternative energy research, and hide how many work-related deaths occur at refineries (possibly as many as six thousand between 2003 and 2005, counting contractors; 2007 set a record for refinery failures). These deaths often occur after repeatedly cited safety violations, accidents, maintenance delays, and legal actions. After the *Valdez* spill in 1989, ExxonMobile told cleanup workers they were safe even though oil in the air exceeded federal standards by four hundred times. After failing to report well over six thousand cases of upper respiratory infections, the company lobbied to avoid having the spill designated as a cleanup of hazardous waste. BP is still trying to emulate these plutonic tactics of deception and secrecy after the disastrous Deep Horizon spill in 2010. Chevron alone employs three hundred in-house lawyers and a litigation budget of $100 million annually. It uses four hundred and fifty law firms globally: a necessity for a com pany responsible for more than ninety active Superfund sites.

Around the world, indigenous people fight for survival against these companies. The Huastecs of Veracruz, the Osages and Poncas of Oklahoma, and the Ogoni of the Niger Delta have all been displaced by Shell, whose private cables brag about having installed agents in key government posts. Protesting Nigerians of Opia and Ikenyan have been attacked by Chevron-leased helicopters. The Acehnese of Indonesia were fired on by troops under Suharto, and Burmese villagers were tortured and enslaved by a junta supported by Unocal (now Chevron). The Kichwa of Sarayaku, Ecuador, were poisoned by oil drilling performed by ConocoPhillips. The Gwich'in of Alaska and Amazonians have been exposed to toxic waste by Texaco (now Chevron). The costs such people are forced pay include genocide, rape, kidnapping, murder, torture, starvation, illness, interference in local governments, displacement of families and towns, and burning down of villages.

As all this goes on, world temperatures increase, oceans rise, the displaced look for new places to live, and the fate of every species on Earth hangs in the terrible balance. A ride in Charon's ferry is not cheap.

In some mythologies, everything is reversed in the Underworld. To extract petroleum from the depths in order to burn it throws into reverse the great geochemical cycles that built life on this planet. Plants and diatoms that poured oxygen into the air took its carbon down into the earth for safe storage. This cleared the way for other forms of life, including ours. When internal combustion (now there's a metaphor!) releases carbon back into the atmosphere, the wheel of evolution on which all life depends spins backwards toward entropy, degeneration, and death. No wonder Yokuts in the Great Central Valley once used petroleum to make death masks.

NOT FAR FROM BAKERSFIELD, the citizens of Taft had held an "Oildorado" festival in honor of the moonscape carved out by their drillers and builders. I drove over to the West Kern Oil Museum to learn more.

The museum turned out to be a replica of the type of oil company that had colonized southwestern Kern County during the early to mid-1920s. As I strolled around inspecting rusting altars of old pipes, pumps, and other contraptions, I could imagine tight-faced, firm-jawed men like Daniel Plainview (*There Will Be Blood*) striding across these barren fields to make a pitch to locals eager for new industry: "I am an oilman, ladies and gentlemen..."

Oil has a way of providing temporary wealth, only to vanish it away, and had done that here too. Buena Vista Petroleum got its start here in 1863 as a source of kerosene and axel grease. Seven thousand derricks pounded and sucked across twenty-five miles through Maricopa, Reward, Midway Valley, Elk Hills; yet McKittrick and Taft had dried up by the late 1960s. A plaque at the museum recalled etymological origins:

> The sturdy derrick, best known of an oilfield symbol owed its name and presumably its origin to an Englishman named Derrick, who, in the 1600, built the forerunners of the oilfield structure to carry out his assigned task, which was hanging people.

One of the remaining derricks stood above me as I looked upward through its red scaffolding at the sky. Known as Jameson #17, it sat on three acres—now eight—purchased to house a museum to an oil boom gone bang. Even so, half of California's exported oil still flows from here, especially the Midway Sunset field still going since 1890.

Taft was founded thirty miles southwest of Bakersfield as an oil depot on the Sunset Railroad. At one time Standard Oil was headquartered here. The town's original name, Moro, got confused with Morro Bay, so someone added an "n." The Ku Klux Klan had done well here; perhaps they too favored the derrick imagery. By the 1960s Standard Oil had relocated and Taft, having been renamed in the 1920s after the "Dollar Diplomacy" president who did nothing to stop widespread lynchings of African Americans, celebrated its proud history with help from the Oildorado Queen and the Maids of Petroleum.

Between the pit and the roads stands a monument,
with a plaque affixed, which says, "AMERICA'S
MOST SPECTACULAR GUSHER." It's a
California Registered Historical Landmark. If you
squint, it could be a gravestone. Around here they
talk about this gusher as if it had a life and an identity, the great creature who sprang forth, lived its
wild existence for a year and a half, and suddenly
died, of subterranean causes.

– James Houston

The reference is to the Lakeview Gusher, one of the worst oil
spills in U.S. history. The oil company from which the well was
named punched a hole in the ground on March 14, 1910 and released
almost nine million barrels of crude onto the landscape. The well
gushed for eighteen months.

West of Taft stretched the Carrizo Plain named after its marsh
reeds. Although it remained the largest native grassland in
California, its center, Soda Lake, was a bowl of salt. The San Andreas
Fault ran cracking along the surface. La Llorona, the folkloric
specter who always seems to haunt sites of colonization and conquest, had been spotted wailing and weeping out here.

At the museum I paused to consider an omega-shaped pipe
wrapped in what looked like crinkled aluminum. EXPANSION
LOOPS the display card informed me. These allowed steam-carry-
ing pipes to expand without breaking. The steam was to force the
petroleum to the surface. The shape reminded me of something I
could not bring to mind. Glancing at photographs of famous oil
platforms, some offshore, I exited to make my way across lifeless
ground on which piles of oil industry junk sat gathering sandstone
dust.

On my way out I had seen an exhibit featuring, of all things, a
crowd of stuffed mice. The real mice had arrived in 1926 when
Miller and Lux diked Buena Vista Lake, formerly one of the largest
bodies of water west of the Mississippi, to plant maize and barley.
The mice loved these crops and bred happily, the more so after the

departure of the heavily hunted hawks and coyotes that had kept
the rodents in check. A heavy rain brought them right into the nearby Honolulu Oil Company, then into other nearby oil operations,
then into Maricopa, Ford City, Taft, El Hills, and Tupman. Cats and
traps having proved ineffective against the onslaught, thousands of
tons of poisoned grain were distributed. By January of 1927, the U.S.
Bureau of Biological Survey sent out a man with the appropriate
name of Piper. Before he could make much of a dent in a mouse population estimated at above forty million, ravens, hawks, sea gulls,
and other hungry birds descended unexpectedly by the thousands
to mop up.

As though in additional comment on the supposed human mas-
tery of nature, Buena Vista Lake reappeared, sheltered and watered
the incoming birds, and evaporated.

> Despite the dominance of agriculture, an unre-
> solved conflict with nature limns human illusion in
> the vast trough, for this place is no more fully tamed
> than is our own deepest being.
>
> – Gerald Haslam

PERHAPS BECAUSE OF MY visit to the oil fields, the color black stood
out a lot in downtown Bakersfield: black street signs, black
awnings, black lamp posts, black tree fences, black bollards; even
the Koch street clock facing off against a derrick-shaped radio
tower was trimmed in black. A junction box in the Arts district had
been decorated with images of large black ants. An abstract sculp-
ture of piled hollow shapes named *Letters from Home* reminded me of
a hydrocarbon chain.

On Eye Street, *Lady Liberty*, a tall replica funded by PG&E, con-
tended with SWAT PC Computer Repair and a mural of stylized
servicemen folded into an American flag painted to the left of a sign
that announced, "Cocktails." In another mural, striped umbrellas
along a riverbank resembled floating pyramids. All were overshad-
owed by the immense AT&T building.

Eye Street. Eye-shaped expansion loops. Pyramidal images. Blackness everywhere mixed with red, like the draperies and pretentious pillars fronting the hotel where I was staying. The Nile Theater downtown. The first big freight boat in town named *Pride of the Desert*. The long Kern River moistening a dry landscape. As I drove down a hill the details began to click mythologically.

In the Dust Bowl days of the depressed 1930s, refugees from Arkansas, Texas, Oklahoma, and other states desertified by unsustainable agriculture brought a nomadic dose of rural Southern culture into the great belly of California. Some arrived broke but hopeful for farm work, only to find the land already in private hands. Their story was told by John Steinbeck in *The Grapes of Wrath*, a novel banned by the Kern Board of Supervisors, and in "The Harvest Gypsies":

> Here, in the faces of the husband and his wife, you begin to see an expression you will notice on every face; not worry, but absolute terror of the starvation that crowds in against the borders of the camp.

Other newcomers better off came to conquer. As early as the 1800s, cotton planters in the Deep South had moved westward to find fresh soil for their nutrient-draining crops. In 1915, when Nazi U-boats sank shipments of Egyptian cotton and the boll weevil wiped out cotton in South Carolina, the U.S. Department of Agriculture started an experiment in the Kern County town of Shafter. There Wofford "Bill" Camp of South Carolina discovered how to grow Acala, a long-staple cotton, in the Central Valley. White gold joined black as Kern County quickly became the world's largest region for single-crop cotton production.

The feudal-era plantation mentality spread like an invasive weed through the San Joaquin Valley. One of its vectors, Asbury Harpending, "The Father of Kern County," went a step further and perpetrated what came to be known as the Great Diamond Hoax by salting mines and fields. A strong Confederacy supporter, he held a commission in the Confederate Navy and funneled Californian gold into the rebel cause. In 1968, Tenneco Corporation bought out the

Kern County Land Company formed by Tevis, Haggin, and Carr, who owned more than a million acres of management property in California and Arizona. Tenneco was bought by Castle and Cooke, a subsidiary of Dole; by 1991, the firm owned a quarter of the available residential property in Bakersfield and 60% of the commercial acreage.

All in all, it would not be too much to say that the San Joaquin Valley exemplifies, at least in certain cultural, financial, and ecological respects, what the Deep South would have become had the Confederacy won the Civil War.

This, and the terrain ruined by unregulated industrialization, might be why other Californians tend to see Bakersfield as the Valley's toilet, or at best as an outhouse for oil-smeared rubes. But the Crystal Palace, a combination restaurant, memorial, and shrine, protests this dark image by celebrating the life of its founding exemplar, Buck Owens.

At one time Bakersfield was both base and stage for Owens, Merle Haggard, Dwight Yoakam, the Maddox Brothers, Sister Rose, Red Simpson, Tommy Hays, and a new style of country music that was folksy, swinging, honky-tonk, and scornful of the smooth orchestrations and programmed electronics emanating from Nashville during the forties, fifties, and sixties. A son of Texan cotton sharecroppers, Owens settled in Bakersfield in 1951 after working on the radio and as a trucker. His 1963 hit "Act Naturally" was picked up and played by the Beatles. In 1972 he and his Buckaroo band released "Streets of Bakersfield."

> You don't know me but you don't like me,
> You say you care less how I feel
> How many of you that sit and judge me
> Ever walked the streets of Bakersfield...

By every measurable standard, Owens' professional life was a story of ongoing success, from co-hosting *Hee Haw* to owning several radio stations to promoting the careers of other country singers. Red, white, and blue guitars signed by him sold for a thousand dollars. His shiny Pontiac sported imitation pistols and silver dollars.

In 2006, after performing at the Crystal Palace, a club he founded in Bakersfield, he died in his sleep.

Many fans of Owens believe, however, that something went out of his music after the death of band leader and longtime friend Don Rich in 1974. Owens had pleaded with Rich for years to stop riding a motorcycle. Rich died on one while driving to see family in Morro Bay. When Owens could finally bring himself to talk about this loss, he said it had caused the "thunder and lightning" to go out of his music. Nevertheless, by the time of his own death his reputation reached around the world.

The club he founded resembles a slice of Old West town, but painted pink. Signs made to look hand-painted read "Livery Stable," "Owens and Sons Livestock," "Saloon." Life-sized statues of Owens await just inside lacquered wooden doors cut with leaded glass windows. Inside the club, a giant screen presents continual video footage of Owens performances for diners. The videos are inescapable, as I learned when I entered the men's room and saw another monitor.

It was morning, so I filled my plate with scrambled eggs, sausage, and toast from the buffet. As I ate my eyes took in glass cases on the walls around the periphery of the club. Each contained Owens mementos, including concert programs, photographs, and sequined costumes he had worn. Behind the stage I thought I glimpsed the famous Pontiac. As more customers sat down, my ears caught the Valley Southern drawl interspersed with occasional laughter. A booted man on my right ate a few bites of a large cut of steak and left.

After breakfast I spent a few minutes reading some of the tributes to Owens posted in what served the place as a lobby or foyer. Here, they announced, was a local son of whom Bakersfield could feel proud. Here, in spite of "Live Cage Fights" and oil cars running through the center of town, was the home-grown answer to all those sneers and jokes about Bakersfield hicks, Bakersfield filth, Bakersfield lack of intelligence or of culture. The whiff of defensiveness in some of these proclamations saddened me a little. I wondered how Owens had liked being a hero in this Valley version of the Egyptian underworld. In ancient Egypt, the mummified pharaohs had been interred with food, clothing, and glittering wealth. Here rhinestones replaced diamonds, bulletins hieroglyphs, and petroleum embalming oil.

Egyptian myths sometimes combined gods who had shared stories: self-created Ammon, protector of roads, and creative Ra, bright god of the sun, or Ra with Set, his hero and shipmate in the celestial barque. Bright gods so often need less luminous twins because the principles they represent interact to produce what neither could attain to alone. Remove one of the pair and the other languishes. Had that happened with Owens and his long companion of concerts and road tours? A companion equipped during one period of Buckaroo fame with an unvarnished black guitar?

Since entering the Valley I could not recollect any dreams. This absence would hold throughout all my explorations here. I wondered whether the exhausted soils and plants were too tired to host any dreams. No vertical depth, just spreading horizontality under tule fog chimeras and hardpan below the surface. It was as though some flattening of dreams had transformed the Valley itself into a dream, shifting, unreal, surreal, misty, dust-deviled, and forever alchemical.

ON MY WAY NORTH, PASSING a Masonic temple, Horace (Horus) Mann Avenue, an omega-shaped eye shining from a psychic's business sign, and Oildale, I made my way to a central fact and presence of the surrounding geography and therefore its psychic core: the Kern River.

This river, the state's third longest at one hundred and sixty-four miles, still possesses its essential wildness even after all its diversions and dammings. Named by John Fremont after topographer and artist Edward Kern, who nearly drowned trying to cross it (Garces had to be carried across by the Yokuts), the Kern had been named Rio Bravo (Wild River) by the Californios for its powerful undertow, treacherous sandy bottom, rapid drops, and many drownings. In 1862 it washed out settlers' canals and homes, and

Bakersfield itself five years later. Contrary even in its direction, it flows south rather than west. In the past its drainage fed wetlands and layered much of the southern Central Valley with its rich alluvial soil it now irrigates; today a smelly stretch of it goes by the name of Royal Flush. Despite its failing health, the Nile of the Valley protects the largest cottonwood and willow woodlands left in California.

I stopped in Hart Park to catch the Kern in a calm mood. I was curious what it thought about as it meandered through a place where "the topography of the land," according to Gerald Haslam, who had grown up in Oildale, "is rarely far from the topography of the soul." Still green in December, the cold park stood almost deserted.

When I knelt on a damp bank I saw rocks in the water under circling islands of foam. The flow bubbled and rushed around and over reeds and smooth stones. Dark silt glittered with tiny flecks of gold. Ducks, twigs, and dead leaves floated by. I put my fingers in the water and closed my eyes, alternating my focus between inner and outer, river and imagination, my heart in the middle to mediate.

At first the river felt and sounded... "tired" somehow, but with enough vitality in it to support birds and other life, including thirsty humans occupying a big chunk of Southern California. I could feel how far the river had come. A state of reverie took hold of me and deepened.

The Kern, it occurred to me, could feel the full span of its life constantly, birth to maturity to old age, death, and rebirth: not like a dream, but a liquid flow of dream-stuff itself. To stop was to strangle and die, to flow was to live...

As I listened, breathing in the damp air, my view of the river as a passive victim to be saved from ecological destroyers began to dissipate. Instead, as the river spirit came into my body through my fingertips, I felt more riverlike myself.

Instead of what I expected to sense from the wash and immensity going by me, I gradually found myself imagining myself from the Kern's point of view—linear, transitory, mortal—and, through that, better able to appreciate the river as its own being apart from the human world. The awful, ancient objectivity of the waters made me want to pull my hand back even while desiring to feel more.

For the Kern, perhaps for every river, its origins, its many currents and eddies and channels, its temperature changes, rises, falls, dips, curves, and losses to damming, drainage, and evaporation form a continual body, a self-regulating whole, diminishable but never divisible. How little we see of our own temporary flux compared to that of the rivers we use, redirect, sometimes pause to appreciate. The Nile, not the pharaohs, founded Egypt, and the same with the Kern and the San Joaquin Valley.

BEFORE LEAVING KERN COUNTY I stopped briefly in Delano, a town named after a man whose first name had been Columbus. Two state prisons sat nearby, with a third up the road in Corcoran. Like many Valley towns, Delano had been given over to mechanized agriculture, a harsh recipe for unemployment rates of over 50% during economic downturns.

Mechanization has never replaced manpower entirely. Almost every fruit and vegetable eaten in the U.S. is picked by farmworkers: two million laborers in this country (almost five million if we count their families), nine hundred thousand of whom are immigrants. Although they work to feed the world while producing $200 billion in agricultural products a year, farmworkers breaking their backs in pouring rain or blistering sun, stooping fourteen to sixteen hours a day to pick berries, fruits, nuts, cut flowers, strawberries, kiwi, herbs, and more than two hundred and fifty specialty crops, do not receive the basic legal and health protections provided to other laborers. When FDR called for the New Deal in the 1930s, the Associated Farmers, the state Chamber of Commerce, the Farm Bureau Federation, PG&E, Southern Pacific, California Packing Association, and Bank of America lobbied to keep farmworkers from inclusion in worker protection legislation.

As they pick, weed, prune, irrigate, clean produce, and stoop under heavy sacks, they get sprayed by pesticides (some of which alter genes and cause cancer), lose toes to frostbite and fingertips to sharp blades, shiver in camps with no hot water, scurry under cover when the camps are bulldozed or set on fire. Crew leaders in the fields beat them, rape them, extort money from them, underreport their work hours, fire them at whim. For workers who cross the international border, dangers include being attacked, robbed, raped, and left to die in the desert or to drown in the Rio Grande by "coyotes" paid to transport them into the U.S. Coyote fees can take indentured families years to work off.

Yet for harvests, farmworkers receive only piecework rates. What pay they manage to collect shrinks to pay for meals, water, tools, and transportation as workers and their children sleep in cars, ditches, plywood huts, and tents stitched together from garbage bags. Because families must migrate with the harvests, schooling for the young remains sporadic. Each year twenty-four thousand children are injured from farmwork and three hundred die from work-related incidents. Those who survive usually miss too much school to ever catch up.

As Daniel Rothenberg, who worked among their families, observed,

> What I found most surprising was that the subterranean world of farmworkers existed side by side with the America I had grown up in—shopping centers, fast-food restaurants, multiscreen movie theaters, convenience stories. I visited frightened, underpaid workers housed in shacks a stone's throw from golf courses, malls, and pristine retirement communities, complete with artificial lakes and fountains.

All this is a direct result of the mass industrialization of food, centralized, top-down, and large-scale. According to Kevin Conway, a San Joaquin Valley grower,

> We're in business to make money and bankrupt our competitors. That's why we exist. We don't exist

for the benefit of the farming community. We don't give a damn about the farming community. We don't believe in promoting agriculture in general, so that all may benefit. We believe in promoting our label.

Although his operation has been investigated several times by the U.S. Department of Labor and repeatedly sued by California Rural Legal Assistance, his attitude and feudalistic management style are not exceptional in the Valley. Seventy-five percent of the nation's vegetables come from 6% of these big farms; 10% of the nation's growers sell 80% of its fruit. The growers consistently fight legislation to improve the lot of workers, and they continue to benefit from the fact that too many laborers looking for work drives down pay. On average workers earn about 1/100th of the sale price of the produce they harvest. Growers earn about 1/3.

One farmworker summed it up concisely: "To them, you're just a machine to get food off the tree."

Racists pretending to be patriots believe that farmworkers are enemies of the state who steal American jobs. Yet no one seems to be lining up to be one of three hundred thousand workers who get sick from pesticides every year, or to spend old age with wrecked minds and broken bodies.

> My husband works the grapes in Delano, California....The farmers use lots of chemicals and sprays, which irritate my husband's eyes, nose, and throat. Sometimes he gets sick. His nose bleeds. He coughs up blood. My husband leaves work each day beaten and exhausted. He's now fifty-eight years old.

As another worker explains,

> We don't want our children to work the way that we've had to work, to suffer what we've suffered.

We want our children to have toys and new shoes, and to study as much as they can. We want them to learn to speak English so that they can find good jobs. We don't want our children carrying a picking sack to the orange groves.

Yet another adds, "We haven't come here to take things away from the Americans. We've come here to contribute. We don't live on public assistance. Our people come here to work."

I spoke to a Central Valley high school and community college instructor who works with students from migrant families and whose father had worked in the fields to put himself through college. My questions are italicized:

Have employment conditions for farmworkers improved in the last two decades?

Not much. Growers like J.G. Boswell block the labor unions from helping people, and medical care usually isn't available. Wages are about the same.

What are the main obstacles to improvement?

The agricultural machine. No medical benefits or treatment. Most small business farmers are gone. School is hard when workers must hold down two or three jobs while raising kids and barely making rent.

What health conditions do you notice in your students?

Respiratory problems, tool injuries, dehydration, lack of sleep, hunger, and Valley Fever [coccidioidomycosis: a fungal infection that causes rashes, joint pain, flu-like symptoms, skin sores, and, in severe cases, pneumonia, meningitis, and death].

How young are farmworkers?

They start when big enough to drag a bag of cotton or haul a crate of oranges.

What environmental risks do they face?

Pesticides—no warning; sometimes they spray when workers are still in the fields. Hot summers, dehydration, on-site fatalities.

Where do most workers live while on the job?

Some employers and work areas provide minimal housing of poor quality. Otherwise workers sleep in cars when they can.

What would you say to people who maintain that illegals are sucking wealth out of this country, eliminating jobs for Americans, and being a burden on healthcare?

Immigrants built this country! Demonizing a group is un-American. Also, food costs would skyrocket, and availability of some foods would plummet, because our style of life depends on farmworker labor. Workers pay for what low-income healthcare is available for them.

What specifically could be done to improve things for farmworkers?

A decent living wage, oversight of pesticides, more managerial power in the hands of the workers (they rarely move up to higher-paying positions), stopping ongoing educational cuts.

"The tragedy of our nation's farmworkers," writes Rothenberg, "lies not in their difference from other Americans but rather in their great and overwhelming similarity." A similarity slated to deepen as contracted labor goes mainstream among America's other employers, more and more of whom outsource jobs, cut back on healthcare when they offer it at all, and let employees go before retirement can begin.

In 1975, the California Agriculture Labor Relations Act signed by Governor Jerry Brown offered the first and only legislation to give farmworkers the right to collective bargaining. In spite of this, grower opposition allied with two subsequent Republican administrations shrunk the United Farm Workers Association (UFWA) from a hundred thousand to ten thousand members. "When I visit workers in their homes," reports Dolores Huerta, co-founder of the UFWA, "I feel as if I'm back in the fifties when we started. People are still being exploited in the same way: little kids carrying twenty-five pound buckets; twenty workers sharing a house just to pay the rent; women who have to meet the foreman in a hotel to get a job.... My anger doesn't make me cynical because we have a solution, a way to change things, a formula—organization."

Huerta had worked with Cesar Chavez, father of two and ex-Navy. His mother and father had been kicked off their Arizona ranch during the Depression, forcing the family to work in the fields. Chavez never went to high school and was shy and soft-spoken, but one day he refused to sit in the "colored" section of the Delano Theater. For this he was arrested and jailed briefly. He emerged determined to fight injustice.

A five-year strike starting in 1965 against table grape growers brought workers a union contract and set the stage for later labor actions, including the formation of the UFWA, popularization of its organ *Malcriado*, informative community drama courtesy of Luis Valdez's El Teatro Campesino, Robert Kennedy flying in to celebrate the end of Chavez's fast for nonviolence, and a "perigrinación" march for rights to Sacramento. If anything, smears of "socialism" by growers willing to accept bracero labor, favorable laws, and huge government subsidies only popularized the movement; by 1980, as its victories extended beyond the Valley, UFWA membership exceeded forty-five thousand, and unionized workers received higher pay, fresh water, toilets, and, in some cases, even medical care and vacation time.

In alchemical symbolism, Chavez and Huerta ruled like Sol and Luna, the King and Queen who oversee the Great Work. The banner of their organization bore the three key colors of alchemy: red, white, and black. The banner's black eagle also flies through alchemy. A medieval woodcut depicts this bird enfolding a couple from behind. The eagle denotes royalty ("Caesar") and spirit, its darkness the *nigredo* or blackening of the Prime Matter at the start of the opus.

As it blackens, the work sometimes falls apart, its spirit flown away. In the Valley this decline is aided by the buzzards, ravens, Clark's crows, and vultures noted by writer Mary Austin on her way through: scavengers known to alchemy as symbols of necessary decomposition.

Why did the campaign for migrant rights begin to decline in the mid-1980s? Some say Chavez was too autocratic and his union too centralized; others, that conservative Californian politicians like Nixon (deep in cahoots with the corrupt Teamsters Union), Deukmejian (who discontinued the environmental cancer research at McFarland), Reagan (who despised activists and encouraged corporatism) and Wilson (who won elections with TV ads of actors impersonating stampeding migrants). According to Richard Castillo and Richard Garcia, "Chavez did not change: conditions changed" as an era of narcissism inflated like a bubble over America. Perhaps it was internal division: key leaders quit over disagreements with Chavez on what direction the union should pursue. Perhaps he had overused the boycott, which he imposed again in 1984; certainly grapes continued to sell despite all his attempts to educate the public about pesticides. Perhaps he spent too much of his energy trying to influence legislators.

Or was it that Chavez, who protested overt injustice so thoroughly, never questioned authorities whose influence he took for granted?

Philosopher and psychoanalyst Felix Guattari offered a useful distinction—based on years of feverish activism in France—between *group-subjects* and *subjected groups*. Subjected groups, because of having been subjected to someone else's dominance, tend to define themselves in reaction to other groups. They enforce traditional roles, norms, hierarchies, power relations, and even modes of exclusion. They often structure themselves around an internalized institution whose values are never called into question, and by doing so, gain for group members a second-hand feeling of immortality. By contrast, group-subjects discover their own internal laws and norms and projects. Acting in relation to other groups, they open themselves to their own evolution, questioning goals along the way. Accepting their own transience, group-subjects make use of "transitional fantasies" to transcend the group through self-directed actions and unorthodox "transverse" communication pathways between various subgroups.

Although the UFWA under Chavez possessed characteristics of group-subjects, including a capacity for inventing their own symbols of identity, one could argue that his circle also behaved—as so many activist groups tend to do—as a subjected group as well. It is never easy to outgrow the mental conditioning of the dominant culture. A lifelong Catholic in the footsteps of his mother and grandmother, Chavez nurtured a religious devotion that some compared to real sainthood. For him, the policies of the church were divine finalities, not human inventions. When he visited the missions of California, he did so to recuperate, not to learn their shadowy history of violent genocide. He never realized the extent to which the church's long colonial history had set up entire peoples, including his own, for lives of subjugation and misery. He accepted support from those priests and nuns willing to offer it with no sense of historical irony or outrage.

Some of his goals for the labor movement reflected this implicit acceptance of entrenched authority. Farmworkers should be paid fairly, should receive food and clean water for their efforts, should be treated as brothers, receive medical attention, and have decent places to live—but the system of agriculture that produced systematic injustice by depending on forced labor, with people compelled to behave like machinery ground on without interrogation. The union's aim was fairer rulers, not to live without any rulers at all.

Losing his mother and then his old friend and mentor Fred Ross took a great toll on his worn-out body. Having done so much to fight for farmworker rights in Delano, Salinas, the Imperial Valley, and so many other places, Chavez was doing the same when he died in San Luis, Arizona, not far from where his family had lost his farm to a bank. He was battling Bruce Church Incorporated, one of the world's largest lettuce growers; ironically, they had bought his family's old property from the bank that had foreclosed it. They had been suing the UFWA for years, and after days in court, Chavez, still fasting, died while reading a book of Native American art. In the opinion of most, he died of overwork.

Chavez made a start (black eagle). A long, dark night of the American soul was at hand with the "conservative revolution" enabled by rich Democrats, the installation of multinationals, the consolidation of the mass media, and unprecedented amounts of wealth being shifted upward from where they supposedly trickled down again. Chavez has been gone since 1993, but the light he struck in the darkness has never guttered out, not even in the depths of *nigredo*, *mortificatio*, or *putrefactio* overshadowing the world's longest, widest, and flattest conglomeration of agricultural machinery.

INTERSTATE 99 HAD BEEN coated in asphalt about the time the Great Delano Grape Strike broke out in 1965. The black pavement moaned beneath my wheels as I drove north toward Tulare County.

Alchemy's essence is transformation. I had known that even before making my way up the Grapevine and into Queen Calafia's state-spanning alchemical vessel. Now I knew it inwardly. From the moment my eyes scanned the barren and destroyed plains below Panorama Drive in Bakersfield, an inner blackening had begun to creep into me. Behind it rose Sol Niger, the powerful, terrible Black Sun of alchemy, whose impenetrable beams brought a dark enlightenment to bear on the work.

All throughout my California investigations I had harbored a quiet hope that all the trauma and damage I witnessed might be reversed somehow. Perhaps enough attention, greenery, permaculture, knowledge, and love could repair these broken landscapes. Perhaps their remaining inhabitants could understand how deeply these places got inside the mind, and from this transition from being spectators, bystanders, enablers, or exploiters into active support- ers and caring dwellers. I still hoped that.

But I had believed all along that I would play some part, if only a modest one, in the regeneration of my homeland.

From atop that Bakersfield overlook, what remained of this hope was sucked away from below into miles of gray pipelines that divid- ed the dry land for as far as I could see. I was done here. I would visit again—in fact I had to in order to finish my California soulseeing— but I was not the man to attempt any renewal in this part of the state. Realizing this felt like what I imagined a husband must go through to accept at last that his wife, whom he married in good faith, was too psychotic to live with, and that helping her was beyond all his powers no matter how much he still loved her. *Separatio.*

The alchemists of times gone by would have understood this in their own chymical fashion. Their writings warned that at some point in the labor, the Prime Matter decomposes and dies. Alchemical woodcuts and manuscripts brim with images of rotting skeletons and dismembered kings. The loss is real, the decay irre- versible. The opus, however, goes on.

Tulare (*ablutio*)

Once upon a time Gylfi, King of Sweden, gave some land to a wandering woman who had entertained him. His gift included as much land as she could plow in a day and a night with four oxen. He did not realize, however, that she was no mortal entertainer, but a goddess of the Aesir, the Norse counterpart to the Greek Olympians, and that her true name was Gefion, "She Who Gives." The oxen were her sons, the offspring of a giant, and with them she transported enough earth to make the island of Zealand. Where the earth had been removed she left a great lake, to Gylfi's lasting awe.

Had she performed this feat in California, the body of water she left behind would have gone by the name Tulare Lake. Commander Pedro Fages named it thus (pronounced "to Larry") after the thick stands of cattails growing around it in 1772 as he rode past looking for deserters from mission outpost duty.

At one time Tulare Lake spread over seven hundred and ninety square miles, the largest inland lake in the West. Yokuts made mats, bowls, and boats from the tules and ate the nutritious sprouts. Settlers took fish from the lake and turtles from marshlands that fed incoming fowl. Everything, it would seem, found its natural containment there, including the Kern, Tule, Kaweah ("gah-WEE-ah"), and Kings Rivers that ended there after descending from the Sierra

Nevada, until the Boswell family, chased by the boll weevil out of Georgia in the 1920s, drained the lake to make room for their new cotton plantation.

Curious about the sources of Aesir power, Grylfi decided to visit their capital. Disguising himself as a traveler named Gangleri, he went forth on a trip that took him at length to what seemed to be Asgard, whose name means "enclosure of the Aesir." Four rivers of milk ran through it. In an immense palace whose roof was composed of battle shields, Grylfi introduced himself as Gangleri, whereupon he was escorted into the presence of three enthroned men, with High seated on the lowest, Just-As-High on that of middle height, and Third on the highest. Odin, himself a shapeshifter, had been known to call himself by those names. The three figures answered Grylfi's questions at length about the gods, the Nine Worlds, and the creation and end of reality.

Snorri Sturlusson's *Prose Edda* heads this story with the title *Grylfaginning*, "Mocking of Grylfi," to make the preservation of Norse myths acceptable to Christian audiences. Grylfi did not really see Asgard or speak to Odin, he was tricked. That is why the tale ends with a clap of thunder that leaves Grylfi alone on a wide, flat plain, the palace and the gods having evaporated from view. Reframing "pagan" myths as all-too-human tales, a revisionism common in Christian retellings, is itself an evaporation, but an incomplete one, leaving the hearer suspecting that the tale would have no point unless Grylfi really was in Asgard and really heard about the nature of divine reality.

Likewise Tulare Lake, gone during dry spells but back again, shimmering and reflective, in times of unexpected flooding. In Yokuts "Kaweah," one of the rivers feeding Tulare Lake, means "Cry of the Raven," the far-seeing, far-flying bird of all-seeing Odin.

VISALIA'S ORIGINAL NAME WAS Four Creeks, though of water and not milk. They fed a magnificent oak forest comparable to that of mountain-straddling Asgard. Not far east of here towers Sequoia National Park, which is why images of forest below high mountains appear in murals painted on the sides of downtown banks.

In Asgard the gods erected a never-finished wall to protect the celestial inhabitants; in Visalia a fortress never to prove its worth stood temporarily over a settlement on the banks of the Kaweah. In Asgard the rainbow bridge Bifrost ("bay-vurst") led to the halls of the gods; in Visalia Bridge Street ends in a suburban cul-de-sac. Asgard was the capital of the Nine Worlds, Visalia of Tulare County. *Asgard* refers to an "enclosure" or a word meaning "grasp"; *Visalia*, named by settler Nathaniel Vise after Visalia, Kentucky, a city whose government evaporated in 2006, probably refers to a "vise." "Vise" in turn goes back to "vine" and "that which binds or winds." "Fresno" refers to an ash tree. When the Norse cosmos was founded, the first man was named Ask after an ash tree, the first woman Embla after a vine. Fresno and Visalia?

The rapid gait of Svadlifari ("Unlucky Traveler"), the stallion father of Odin's horse Sleipnir, had helped raise the wall around Asgard before the trickster Loki showed up as a mare to lure Svadlifari away. By the mid-1850s, travelers traded tired mounts for fresh in Visalia, home of the light Visalia Saddle, and by 1858, the Butterfield Stage stopped there regularly. During the Civil War, Visalia remained so pro-Confederate that locals stole horses and gave them to the Rebel forces.

I saw no signs of those days when I drove into town through a downpour and parked in front of one of the forest murals. With an umbrella over my head I stooped to read the title: *Big Trees*. In two murals rivers ran below snowy peaks.

As in Asgard, and as in other Edenic places where four sacred rivers meet, flows still join in this former wetland where the Valley reaches seventy-five miles in width. I saw giant crown on signs as well as "Mineral King / Noble Court," "Crown Jewel of the San Joaquin Valley," "Enchanted Playhouse," and "Sugar Plum's Boutique": joinings of myth to locale. The letter V was prominent: V not only for *Visalia* or "Veouria Records" but for Valhalla, Odin's great hall in Asgard, although here it was "Valhalla Restaurant and Gifts." A V or diamond shape frames Lincoln Oval Park, the oldest section of the city. Just south of it below Main, a sculptured figure reminiscent of the sentinel Heimdal blows a long horn.

Here Mesopotamian, German, Scandinavian, Mission Revival, and Greek Revival architecture runs together, even on single build-ings: in the case of one structure, bricks alternating with singles. On a black awning soaked with rain a large white T shape resembling a hammer reminded me of Thor's.

Why Norse mythology in this part of the Valley? Why Egyptian in Bakersfield?

Myths begin with stories wedded to the presence of the lands in which they originate. The hearer can no more understand Egyptian mythology in any real depth without knowing its sources along the Nile River and in the Valley of the Kings than make sense of proud Athena or Athens without the upthrust of the stony Acropolis, or of warlike Romulus and Remus outside of volcanic Rome. Norse myth began up in forested mountains cut by rivers and streams. Something like it must arise, therefore, in similar terrains.

But because myth contains archetypal motifs found everywhere, their recurrence reaches across pantheons, places, even eras. The Native Californians of the Valley had heard nothing of Norse myth before 1800, if then, but their local deities must have expressed pat-terns and presences similar to the Norse and Egyptian. It's a shame we don't know how. Beyond the Valley in Santa Barbara, St. Barbara intuitively imaged the seaside abode of the Wisdom Goddess known to other cultures as Sophia, Brigid, and Mary. To the Chumash she was Hutusch, wise weaver of the rainbow bridge stretching out to the Channel Islands. Wisdom Goddess motifs like gazes downward from on high, luminous depths, and cultural edu-cation have played out for millennia in St. Barbara's town even before it was a town, its treasures tucked between the sparkling blue Pacific and the Santa Ynez Mountains.

I took refuge from the storm in a small storefront restaurant jammed with copper pipes, tanks, and other apparatus built to dis-till fermented beverages. Unlike the warriors tipping brews eternal-ly in Valhalla, I had never acquired a taste for beer or mead, so I sipped coffee instead. From the open doorway a draft (the inevitable word) cooled the overheated interior. I pictured John Steinbeck, wet and enraged, stacking sandbag walls on the edge of town in a downpour in the 1930s. After working all night to protect homeless families arrived from the South, he fell fast asleep in the mud. I shook my head, sipped. *Where is Svadlifari when you need him?*

After blackening comes whitening. Alchemists used the words *albedo* and *ablutio* to describe the purification of the Prime Matter after calcination and putrefaction had blackened it. The adepts washed it in a flask; here rain and flood did their cleansing work within the Tulare Basin.

Container, condenser, confluence, enclosure, vise, vine. Tulare County shares Kings Canyon National Park with Fresno County to the north, Mount Whitney with Inyo County to the east, and the Kings River and part of Tulare Lake's basin with Kings County to the west. Containers brimming with milk brought more revenue to the county every year than any other source except agriculture. Since 1968 the World Agricultural Exposition has gathered in Tulare the city, a former repair depot for the Southern Pacific.

This place of gathering also grew the seeds of strife. Many of the first officials of Tulare County came to violent ends. Mayor James Savage was killed by Judge Arvey, Alonzo Edwards by Bob Collins, Dr. Everett, the assessor, by a man named Bell. In fact, all but two of the first set of officers were murdered: California Ragnarok, where polarized opposites eliminated each other.

In 1861, President Lincoln relieved Albert Sidney Johnston from his command of federal troops in California. Johnston, who owned a ranch in what is now Pasadena, eventually served Jefferson Davis as lieutenant-general. He was not alone. In the Valley, where Southern plantation owners had successfully relocated, so much pro-Confederate sympathy stirred that General Wright of the Union ordered the postmasters of California to stop distributing the *Stockton Argus*, the *Stockton Democrat*, the *Stockton Republican*, the *Merced Banner*, the *Merced Democrat*, the *Merced Express*, the *Visalia Post*, and the *Visalia Equal Rights Expositor*. The *Mariposa Free Press* also leaned toward the South. It was understood if not spoken that "equal rights," "states' rights," and "free" referred to a ruling class of white people. In Visalia citizens staged a Civil War in miniature on Main Street.

Throughout the San Joaquin Valley in the second half of the eighteenth century, land grabs supported by federal colonization laws brought war with the Native Californians and conflict between farmers and ranchers over water and territory. By 1871, five hundred and sixteen men owned nine million acres. Miller alone would control 1.3 million acres, nine hundred thousand of it in the San Joaquin Valley, and more than a hundred thousand head of cattle. The labor force required to do all this increasingly mechanized work within the long California alchemical container reflected a broad diversity of human components:

> The Armenians and their raisins, the Slavs and their table grapes, the Basques and their sheep, the Azores Portuguese and their milk cows, Swedes in Kingsburg, Filipinos in Delano, Punjabis in Caruthers and Asyrians in Turlock. The Dutch Reformed, German Mennonite, White Russians, German Russians, Hmong, "Mexicans, Chinese, Japanese, dirty knees."
> – Mark Arax and Rick Wartzman

Container, condenser, confluence, enclosure, vise, vine. In Tulare County, the vine that bound up an empire took the form of cotton.

The empire began with "Colonel" Boswell's transplantation of his cotton operation from Georgia to California in the 1920's and was fed by his marriage into the infamous Chandler dynasty of Los Angeles. What he passed down to his nephew, J.G. Boswell, had grown into the largest industrialized cotton plantation in the world. Supplemented by extensive seed alfalfa, safflower, and wheat crops, it spread into Kings and Fresno Counties and on into Arizona, Colorado, and Oregon. Arax and Wartzman:

> King Cotton. It enriched Alexandria, spurred irrigation in the Sudan, brought fame to Shanghai and became woven into the Indian cultures of Peru, Guatemala and Mexico. It attired the army of Alexander the Great, caught the eye of Pliny the

Roman and drew raves from sixteenth-century English botanist John Gerard, who said of its seed oil: "It taketh away many freckles, spots and other blemishes of the skin." It triggered Britain's Industrial Revolution, which pulled people away from their home looms and into the cities with their sweltering factories—the fodder for Karl Marx's *Das Kapital*.

J.G. Boswell of Corcoran proved as ambitious as his uncle. Although he felt no interest in farming, he was driven to compete. Whether fishing, playing cards, hunting, hiking, or growing his empire, he had to stay on top, always win, come in first. Those who did not were "losers," "wussies," and "whining weaklings." According to his son, Boswell, who shamed the young man publicly, ran his cotton business on "fear and intimidation." Even his transparent lies—about winning a varsity letter at Stanford, about working on his crushed fingers with a scissors—propped up his macho image. He liked to drink whiskey from an old body lotion bottle that his wife gave him.

Like many empire rulers he was secretive about much that he did. "As long as the whale never surfaces," he liked to explain, "it is never harpooned."

Corporatists like to emphasize the social benefits of large-scale operations. Boswell helped developer Del Webb build his Sun City communities. The Boswell empire gave millions of dollars to local groups like the YMCA, founded baseball fields, paid for a high school, supported local vendors. Its food crops, including tomatoes, fed millions. Its cotton crops clasped wearers all over the world in warm garments. The company funds environmental groups, farms with robots and satellite technology, implements Integrated Pest Management to reduce pesticide use. Yet even in J.G.'s day, shanty-towns of plywood were going up in the San Joaquin Valley. Despite corporate contributions Corcoran slides downhill, its manpower replaced by mechanization, its busted unions stillborn. In bad years one of four residents of Kings County live in poverty, with an unemployment rate of 16% in Corcoran. In the early 1960s, Boswell, a long-time backer of the Associated Farmers, blocked local laws to build low-income housing for immigrants by calling this "socialism"; but of $23 million in federal crop subsidies collected since 1996 by seven local growers, not a penny went to the fruit, vegetable, or nut farms of Kings County.

Cotton requires a lot of water: two hundred and fifty-seven gallons to make one T-shirt. After draining Tulare Lake in the 1920s, the Boswell empire controlled the San Joaquin Valley's four largest rivers and made sure of state and federal legislation favorable to water subsidization. Boswell has also pressured the Department of Fish and Game not to investigate fish kills or rising selenium and toxaphene levels.

Perhaps the most basic attitude of the Boswell operation toward the natural world is set forth in Boswell's pro-grower propaganda film *The Big Land*: "The American farmer has become a giant. No longer does he serve the land. The land serves him." Until it dries up and puffs away. Until salt makes it infertile. Until chemicals kill its microorganisms. Until a flood arrives and Tulare Lake reappears...

From all about me I felt the forces of many convergences. Was it the sight of multiple faces on buildings? The multiculturalism evident in the rain-swept streets? The biodiversity of Visalia, with its sequoias, oaks, hills, rivers, creeks, and abundant native plants? *Albutio* can separate out, but it also irrigates and refreshes complexity. In the end of industrial days, when the breakage of self-contradiction finally shuts down the Age of Empires and its armies, armadas, and automata, cultural and ecological diversity may well hold the center as the only firm ground left to stand on.

Fresno (*arbor philosophorum*)

And since we knew the free way
and how an ugly road was coming,
and how invaders would arrive
with charts instead of hearts,
and since we knew
they would come and be gone,
in dust, in just,
we dusted our selves off
and went inside and out
and wherever we've been
with our families,
spreading the center among us.

– Lawson Fusao Inada, from "California
  Heartland: The Exact Center"

I approached Fresno with trepidation. Reaching outward from the center of California and of the San Joaquin Valley, Fresno County, the nation's agricultural hub, suffers from industrial pollution so severe that one in six children go to school there carrying an inhaler

67

for asthma.

This kind of pollution afflicts the entire Central Valley, indeed the entire state, where all forms of air pollution annually cause nine thousand premature deaths, sixteen thousand hospitalizations, six hundred thousand asthma attacks, 1.7 million cases of respiratory illness, 1.3 million school absences, and five million lost workdays. The top five of the nation's ozone-polluted areas, and eight of the top ten particulate-polluted counties, are found in California.

In the San Joaquin Valley, where dirty air pools, agriculture and sprawl generate invisible particulates that combine lethally with the region's thick fogs. (The Central Valley buys and sprays a third of the pesticides manufactured in the U.S.) Children living in smoggy areas lose 1% of their lung capacity per year. Ultrafine exhaust particles that cause cancer, leukemia, birth defects, low birth weight in babies, bronchitis, and emphysema are not filtered out by car air systems; they accumulate within three hundred feet of freeways and hover even above parked cars, which means that commuters who spend an hour a day on the road are losing years off their lives. In fact, people living near congested freeways are twice as likely to develop cancer as those living next to a factory. Illness numbers connected with diesel-powered machinery are even scarier.

Below the ground, 65% of wells near Central Valley dairies test above the public health limit for nitrates: odorless, colorless contaminants that leak from fertilizer, manure, septic tanks, and even wastewater treatment plants. Nitrates are implicated in Blue Baby Syndrome and in cancers found in lab animals. Over the past decade, more than two million Californians have been exposed to high nitrate levels. State law requires their removal, but rural communities often lack adequate treatment systems, and enforcement is feeble. None of the dairies were fined.

A quarter to half of the wells in Fresno County are also contaminated with DBCP (dibromochloropropane) run off from soil fumigants. This pesticide has been linked with breast and lung tumors and genetic damage. Aldicarb, nitrates, and toxic manure swim in the groundwater of all nineteen Valley counties. Cancer clusters have cropped up in Fowler, McFarlane, and Earlimart, and rates of heart and blood disease and nervous system disorders are rising rapidly. Birth defects have also begun to cluster: in Kettleman City for example, where they have gone as high as sixty-four a year and where Waste Management Inc. runs a toxic waste dump three miles from town.

Fresno's sprawl, urban and suburban density (it is the fifth largest city in California), rising population, and agricultural industry concentrate these afflictions. Ozone, an agent in asthma, heart disease, emphysema, fetal heart problems, and lung acid, pours forth not only from machinery but from cow waste emissions. Smog carries a brown tinge redolent of methane, nitrates, manganese, and carbon monoxide. The nonprofits Earthjustice and Farmworker Justice are demanding that the U.S. Environmental Protection Agency draft regulations to protect children from farm chemicals sprayed near schools. Meanwhile, California's politically compromised Department of Pesticide Regulation has ignored its own scientists to approve methyl iodide, a documented agent of neurological damage, fetal death, thyroid disease, and cancerous tumors of the lungs and brain, for use as a strawberry pesticide. As usual, farmworker health will bear the brunt, but consumers remain largely unaware of the dozens of chemicals that coat the fruit they eat.

Valley Fever has become epidemic; the Centers for Disease Control and Prevention recommend that children and old people wear masks in dusty areas. Of Fresno's two hundred and thirty-four wells, nearly all are polluted to some extent. All this impacts plants too: ozone crop damage alone reaches $150 million a year in the San Joaquin Valley.

Just as lack of regulation permits agricultural and industrial conglomerates to do as they please regardless of declining public and environmental health, so it encourages developers to build without adequate planning or rational restraint. During the 1980s, a dozen Fresno politicians, lobbyists, and developers were checked into the Gray Bar Hotel after being convicted for illegal activities that bloated the county's urban sprawl. Throughout the San Joaquin Valley, a region larger than ten states, population now

exceeds that of twenty. During the 1990s, 53% of ninety-seven thousand paved-over acres had once been prime cropland. Another nine
hundred thousand acres of farmland now face the bulldozer and
cement mixer. By 2040, the loss of agricultural output through land
development could top $860 million a year.

I was less concerned about air, water, or soil pollution during my
relatively brief visits to Fresno than about their psychic impact.
Raised defenses would render me insensitive, but I resolved to carefully monitor my mood, how my body felt, and any dreams that
occurred while I was there (none did). Not that anybody on site
could render me assistance should I need it. Sometimes it's disconcerting to live in a dualistic culture almost totally deaf to the translation of ecological into psychological trauma.

I decided on a flanking approach. Circling around westward to
Interstate 5, I passed through Coalinga.

Coalinga was once the Southern Pacific's Coaling Station A in
the days when locomotives ran on coal. Today the town sits near
two prisons and a Chevron oil field. One of the prisons houses violent sexual offenders. A sign along the freeway states that "*Jesus is
Lord of Coalinga.*" The words float in a cloud beneath a rainbow.

In 1971, Jean Dakessian and her husband hit on a way to direct
visitors to their new motel. She got their attention by painting the
heads of oil derricks to look like animals visible from the freeway. At
one time this "Iron Zoo" included a zebra, goat, beagle, butterfly,
giraffe, ram, and twenty-seven other figures painted by Dakessian
and residents of Coalinga, including the mayor. With the decline in
oil production, derricks began to disappear and deplete the stock of
animals, an event mirrored elsewhere as petroleum-fueled mass
extinction erased real animals from existence.

according to the sign
on the spine of the highway
these hills are lost

irrigation canals

have broken the bones
of foothill and valley....
– Wendy Rose, from "Coalinga"

Coalinga's mood of strangeness might derive in part from the southeast-dropping anticline below its rocky surface. This Kregenhagen-Temblor formation contains shales filled with organic sediments trapped since the Eocene Epoch stretching from 54.8 to 33.7 million years ago. Oddly enough, the Eocene marks the emergence of mammals like those painted on the heads of Chevron pumps. At the end of that epoch, climate change brought a mass extinction named the Grande Coupure ("Great Break").

Did images on the surface of Coalinga recall events of long ago laid down beneath the surface? Events whose awful repetition must impact our species too? In town an attempt at modernization included historic plaques describing buildings no longer there. "Rockwell Building: Built in 1904, Destroyed by Earthquake in 1983." "Pleasant Valley Hotel: Built 1910 - Burned 1935." As in oily Bakersfield, the street signs here were black.

FRESNO AWAITED SIXTY-SIX miles to the northeast. Along I-5, signs posted in front of barren stretches of cropland indicated a "Congress [no hyphen] Created Dust Bowl." Growers whose lobbyists accused social safety net advocates of asking for handouts were fuming about drought-necessitated decreases in their water allotments. Evidently they knew too little history to realize that the Dust Bowl resulted primarily from decades of unsustainable agriculture. Soils protected by composting, cover-cropping, swaling, mulching, and companion-planting don't blow away in the wind.

Had I taken I-99 north from Visalia (which I did on other trips), I would have gone through a town named Selma. All three accounts of the naming of Selma point to someone's daughter. "Selma" means "helmet of God." Could Athena be here in the Central Valley? A mother named Selma some credit for giving her name to the place raised a daughter with the masculine pen name Georges Lewys (real name Gladys Lewis). She was the author who sued Eugene O'Neill for plagiarizing his *Strange Interlude* from her *The Temple of Pallas Athene*. She lost, and lost again when she tried to convince O'Neill's publisher to become her own in exchange for dropping her claims against the playwright.

In 1861, botanist William Henry Brewer passed through what is now Fresno during the first California Geological Survey. He saw one large, dilapidated house, one small house, one barn, one empty warehouse, and a corral. These were circled by rush-covered swamps stretching all the way to Tulare Lake. The barrenness of the Valley "depressed the spirits," Brewer wrote. Proceeding south, his team found an illiterate Secessionist couple with several ragged children living by the Kern River in what is now Bakersfield.

Fresno's American settlement phase began in 1867, when Anthony Easterby bought farm land just south of present-day State Route 180. He wanted to grow wheat, so in 1871, a sheepherder with the religious name of Moses J. Church built Easterby an irrigation canal. Moses must have been skilled at redirecting water because his efforts led to the Fresno Canal and Irrigation Company.

By 1872 a Central Pacific Railroad stop stood near the Easterby farm, which, seedlike, promoted other civic growth. Fresno incorporated in 1885 and became the county seat in 1874 in favor of flood-prone Millerton, inundated by the San Joaquin River on Christmas Eve in 1867. Millerton achieved full baptismal submergence in 1944, when construction of Friant Dam put it under a lake, although what's left of the town reappears when droughts lower the reservoir level. Fresno remained and spread out.

Let the civic seed of Easterby's farm be imagined growing on a surface traced east to west by State Route 180. When the seed sprouts into a tree of human occupation, the southern segment of Route 41 serves it for a trunk. Its northern segment, I-99, and SR 168 form its main branches, as can be verified on a map. Almost all of Fresno's astounding suburban overdevelopment has shot upward from these branches.

The name "Fresno" derives from the Spanish word for the white ash trees lining the San Joaquin River. The tree emblem graces signs all over the city. The ancient Norse would have thought of Yggdrasil, the great ash tree that grows in the center of the Nine Worlds. The alchemists named it the *arbor philosophorum*, the full-fruited Philosophical Tree of their art, its roots deep in dark Prime Matter and its top the perch of the marvelous Philosopher's Stone. An alchemical document unfolds this more:

> All animals, trees, herbs, stones, metals, and miner-als grow and attain to perfection, without being necessarily touched by any human hand: for the seed is raised up from the ground, puts forth flow-ers, and bears fruit, simply through the agency of natural influences. As it is with plants, so it is with metals. While they lie in the heart of the earth, in their natural ore, they grow and are developed, day by day, through the influence of the four elements: their fire is the splendor of the Sun and Moon; the earth conceives in her womb the splendor of the Sun, and by it the seeds of the metals are well and equally warmed, just like the grain in the fields....For as each tree of the field has its own peculiar shape, appearance, and fruit, so each mountain bears its own particular ore; those stones and that earth being the soil in which the metals grow.
>
> – *Gloria Mundi*

The Tree as form is archetypal. Even the human nervous system takes an arboreal shape through evolutionary time, from spinal chord up through brain stem, center, and cortical layers ramifying like branches reaching skyward. Of course we walk upright! "Dendrite" carries the Tree in its name. A cutaway view of the brain resembles cypress and cauliflower.

Little wonder this Tree-themed place has attracted biblical imagery, Christian in particular. Fig Garden Home Owners Association. Christmas Tree Lane towering over a section of Van

Ness Boulevard. Vineyards on Temperance Avenue. A mural titled *Grape Harvest* above the doors of the Post Office on Tulare. In *Planting of Cultures*, a mural on the side of the California State Building, grapevines intertwine generations of happy Fresnoans.

I scrawled travel notes on the maps I had printed out and brought along. Between the western and central branches (99 and 41), strip malls; between 41 and 168, suburbs and malls. Within the downtown, the west sector Mexican, the southwest industrial, south is government, east is business parks, northeast Mexican and Black (also car and beer shops), north is automobile parts and tire shops.

As I drove the streets of Fresno I forced myself yet again to really see the exact sensorial details of urban and suburban sprawl. The geometry of sameness and straightness, with lines of dividers, curbs, sidewalks, building corners and roofs, window edges, and the like, point the eye away to a boundless horizon of opportunity that never appeared. Difficult to resist the numbing impact of signs and facades and logos and labels: McDonald's, Burger King, Check Cashing, Appleby's, Costco, each an invisible hammer striking through the eyes and into the heart, over and over, numbing it and the nervous system that enervates it. Now and again, nature's natural irregularities came into view, perhaps through a jagged leaf or a tree leaning sideways; but by and large, developers and financiers had covered, factoried, this once-free curve of world with a reflective frontier of boxes, panels, and planes. Just seeing it was enough to make the soul want to subside into protective unconsciousness while the eyes, freshly plucked from their weary sockets, cooled off in some handy shirt pocket.

Fresno's population burgeoned throughout the second half of the twentieth century, with the city one of the hundred largest in the U.S. by 1960: population one hundred thirty-four thousand and climbing. In the 1990 census Fresno held forty-seventh place at three hundred fifty-four thousand, and thirty-seventh place by 2000, a 21% increase in residents over the previous decade. In 1995, history repeated itself when the FBI's Operation Re-Zone caught prominent Fresno and Clovis politicians taking bribes in return for rezoning cheaply purchased farmland for suburban growth. Another sixteen for the Gray Bar Hotel, but fifty thousand acres a year continue to be paved in spite of this.

Within the downtown triangle formed by routes 180, 99, and 41, the tree pattern repeated itself at a smaller level of magnification, with Divisadero Street as ground-level crown, vertical streets like trunk and branches above it, and diagonal street-roots reaching below and southward. Here in the very center of California, I stood looking across an intersection converging on cracked pavement ringed round about by Super Suds Laundry, Arco, Auto Depot, and McDonald's. My mood abruptly plummeted. Was *this* after all the very core of my homeland? A shabby, empty junction signifying nothing?

BALDASSARE FORESTIERE CAME TO the U.S. from Sicily in 1901, probably to escape from an overpowering father. In 1906, having roughened his hands and back digging subway tunnels in Boston and New York, he bought acreage in Fresno and began chipping away at the ground. His initial idea was to build an underground resort for visitors eager to escape the heat of a Valley summer.

His pick struck hardpan. He quickly verified that two to six feet of it underlay most of his property. Anyone else would have resorted to dynamite or moved on. Forestiere did neither. Instead, he kept digging.

By 1923, he had dug out ten acres of at least thirty underground rooms, some of which he lived in. One was a ballroom laid out as a compass design. A devout Catholic, he worked the Trinity into his labors: trinities of trees, of rooms; a Trinity Courtyard bearing a ninety-five-year-old grapevine of three productive branchings. He strengthened the walls by lining them with the hardpan he excavated with his simple tools. The entire complex ringed itself outward from a central circular room containing a citrus tree grafted to bear seven varieties of citrus. He also planted wine and table grapes.

In 1946, having received no tourists, he died of a hernia and pneumonia.

Why had Forestiere spent forty hard years of his life digging holes in mineralized clay? No one knows, but an utterance of his might offer some clue: "My visions overwhelm me."

In his underground garden I ducked under rocky arches and passed through caverns. Vines and trees still grew here, many taller for having to reach skyward toward the light. "One Tree: Seven Varieties of Citrus" a plaque informed me. The Philosophical Tree of alchemy bore seven fruits as well, one for each of the planets. The alchemists believed they corresponded with types of metals amenable to transformation into nobler and nobler substances. "As above, so below."

Not everything that lives underground produces good fruit in Fresno. The Fresno Municipal Sanitary Landfill, the first of its kind in the U.S., closed in 1987 but distinguished itself by becoming both a National Historic Landmark and a Superfund site. Miniature pseudo-lakes laid out around town echo the region's runoff-poisoned wells. The land itself is subsiding into depression, literally and imaginally, as much as thirty feet from groundwater pumping. Speaking of Fresno, where what hides below rises one day into full view, "This is a place," noted local poet Corrinne Hales, "where profound truths (both positive and negative) about American life are working themselves out in plain sight every day. In many ways, it seems to me the truest place I've ever lived."

I like to think that by breaking through hardpan, Forestiere also broke through the cultural concrete that smothers the voice of the land. An unknowing alchemist armed with a pickax, he sensed unerringly that some sacred and vital presence hid down below long before its manifestation in cultivated fertility made Fresno the towering Yggdrasil of American agriculture. He himself offered an example of the cultural fertility that raised up a Little Armenia, Little Italy, German Town, China Town, and many other enclaves of diversity throughout the county.

David "Mas" Masumoto operates an organic peach and grape farm twenty miles south of Fresno. (Ninety-nine percent of all U.S. raisins grow just outside of Fresno.) The farm has been in his Japanese American family for three generations. It even survived the imprisonment of Masumoto's parents during World War II. Masumoto practices soil-building methods, engages in "literary farming" (he has written several books), and talks to his trees. After college he came back to the Valley: "I returned to the farm to hear stories."

And to slow down. "As I walk my fields, I stop worrying about irrigation timetables and days to harvest. I force the voices of pesticide salesmen from my mind. I begin to work in silence."

> Natural farming methods require time. Compost takes months, even years, to work into roots and plants. Biological controls (good bugs eating bad bugs) are not quick fixes; generations of lacewings and ladybugs may need to call my farm home before their population levels can challenge worms.

What food tastes like, Masumoto insists, depends on the qualities unique to a place. "Large-scale farming operations can't mimic my methods." He adds: "This archaic method of creating raisins by simply laying grapes on trays in the sun speaks with a language of the past. Slow. Curing. Exposed. Both the raisin and the raisin farmer." To produce literary farming is to tend organic metaphors that bind together people and their place.

> Now I understand why they call these cultural practices. Good pruning is not a science, it's the art of working with a living entity, an annual sojourn to a familiar place with the intention of returning the next year and the year after that... The ghosts of many pruners before me live in my fields—this is a place where generations reside.

The blooming of cultural diversity in the Valley does not imply its unequivocal acceptance. Conservative voices now calling stridently for the deportation of Iranians and Muslims echo the tones heard when the Masumotos and other Japanese families found

themselves behind barbed wire. They were waiting to be freed
when Mas's beloved Uncle George died fighting for the U.S.

Aware of the irony, Masumoto rejects the bitterness of the
chronic victim. Instead, he applies a touch of humorous eco-analy-
sis:

> Hardpan, a metaphor for the Valley. A rock that
> doesn't want to be moved, like the conservative
> politics of this place, where traditions become
> embedded, adaptation often slow, acceptance of
> difference difficult.. Hardpan politics thrive here:
> people have long memories and distrust outsiders,
> often seeking local solutions to problems.

In my book *Storied Lives* I followed up on Jung's discovery of personal myth: the reborn tale we come in with. Jung, for example,
lived the myth of Faust, but his consciousness of his myth transmuted a tragedy into an achievement. Steinbeck lived Lancelot,
even down to a childhood home nicknamed called "the castle," a
wife named *Gwen*, the title of his first novel (*Cup of Gold*), an
attempt to save his friend *Arthur* Miller from the blacklist, and an
unfulfilled quest—in his case to translate Malory's *Morte d'Arthur*
into contemporary American English. His favorite virtue:
"Gallantry." It matters to know one's myth, but it matters more to
work gracefully with what it brings.

I suspect Masumoto's myth is the Japanese figure Momotaro, or
Peach Boy, who came to earth encased in a peach and who won
much wealth and respect for his family after conquering dangerous
ogres. Masumoto confesses to imagining a science fiction film in
which all memory has been prohibited because it hinders progress.
Old orchards and vineyards are destroyed, but he, a heroic mad
peasant, possesses a hidden tree of knowledge. It has the power
through taste to trigger memory and release the poetic soul thereby.
"Of course," writes the author of *Things Worth Savoring* and *Epitaph for
a Peach*, "my tree is always full of fruit." Where better to harvest it
than in a place named after a tree?

I had begun to wonder whether Aphrodite had been cast from the Valley altogether. But when a group of sixth-graders visited Masumoto's farm, and he pointed out to them tiny flowers of shepherd's purse,

> One bright girl picks a handful, tickles her nose with the delicate blooms, and makes a bouquet to take home. She explains, "These are all about love, right? Look at the tiny heart-shaped leaves!" A detail I hadn't noticed before.

He quotes a Chinese proverb: "A bird does not sing because it has the answer, it sings because it has a song."

I WALKED DOWNTOWN AND SAW Armenian, Hmong, and Mexican memorials, and, unexpectedly, a friendly squirrel that ran up chattering for a look at me. *Ratatosk?* A polished stone monument dedicated by the Military Order of the Purple Heart proclaimed alchemically, "My stone is red for the blood they shed..."

I saw shield, leaf, and bough shapes carved into tall old buildings. At the Fulton Mall shopping arcade across the street from Warnors, a theater fronted by horse images with blurred legs and outlines (Sleipnir?), a fountain meandered water from two bronze women with heads together ("The Visit") into basins containing sculpted tree trunks. One eye-shaped piece in a circular fountain looked back at me, reminding me of Mimir's well and the eye Odin left in it as payment for remembrance and deep wisdom. Another fountain held four eyes posted on a vertical axis. A hooded figure in stone recalled Odin himself.

A *Fresno Grizzlies* banner brought to mind Berserkers, the "Bear Shirt" warriors out of Old Norse myth. I could not see Heimdall, but wedding horns were honking there, and again at the Fresno Hotel. More tree artwork of wire and stone, "Treehousing" shouted from a graffiti-like mural, and interlocking circles everywhere: parking garages, fountain bases, pavement markings, Nine Worlds beneath my feet as well as overhead...

> The Central Valley has annealed my spirit. The hard valley light and its dryness is tough and unforgiving. I am not engaged in a romance. My landscape is state buildings and shopping malls, pizzerias and Southeast Asian restaurants. It is a landscape of violation. Yet there is a landscape. In the mornings before the commuters and sirens and leaf blowers, there is an eerie beauty over our mess.
>
> – Fred Dalkey

A bewildering variety of things took root here: the Fresno scraper (capable of filling low spots with soil), the first successful credit card (a bank is still the tallest building in Fresno), popping (a dance style in which waves of energy seem to pulsate through dancers' bodies), "Fresno" the miniseries (a soap opera parody)... and, here in a place favored by Odin, poetry.

It started, at least in modern times, with Fresno native, poet, and playwright William Saroyan, and again with William Everson. The fountain opened wide in 1958, when Philip Levine took up a position as associate professor at Fresno State College. Over two decades he encouraged his students to write poetry and eventually won the Pulitzer Prize for it himself. The group of mentors came to include Peter Everwine, Robert Mezey, David Kherdian, Charles Hanzlicek, Corrinne Hales, Juan Felipe Herrera, Ana Garza, Tom Emery, Liza Wieland...

In 1970 the first anthology of the Fresno Poets reached publication. Two more would follow, with the latest, *How Much Earth*, published in 1999.

> a Chinese merchant
> telling a Japanese boy
> about an Indian man
> playing in a black band
>
> – Lawson Fusao Inada, from "Trombpoem"

I hated high school then, & on weekends drove
A tractor through the widowed fields. It was so
boring
I memorized poems above the engine's monotone...

– Larry Levis, from "The Poet at Seventeen"

That Impersonal 99. And
Not even crosses for the
Dead alongside this road
Of the timeless vanishing
Point.

– Jose Montoya, from "Gabby Took the 99"

Autumn, old mother, you bless with lightning
bolts.
Thunder shudders caprock, rolls down the
canyon...
In town the streets run red with rain....
Do trees listen
to our words as we attend to their thrumming
music?
Mother of all that I remember—
Your rains wash my eyes,
I see the blue earth breathing low and still.
In this soil you gather my family....
In you I learn the rhythm that rises
and fails in my heart.

– George Keithley, from "Autumn"

Delano, MacFarland, Famosa....
I name them and they vanish.
Little towns that have listened
so long to fenders crumpling,

flying glass, to tires unraveling
and men catching fire.

– Greg Pape, from "On Our Way"

Three ants pass
across the back of my reddened
right hand.
Everything is speaking or singing.
We're still here.

– Philip Levine, from "Magpiety"

The ranches I knew as a boy have turned to salt
and winter like my grandmother's unbunned white
hair
haunts the ruins of broken mirrors
in empty stations look for the river back to eden

– baloian, from "Fresno Indian"

Nights, the saws dream of lost fingers...

– Loretta Collins Klobah, from "Storm"

The harmony of West Fresno
comes from sound composition—
the very streets composed
on the scale from "A" to "G,"
with in-between alleyways
shading in sharps and flats.

– Lawson Fusao Inada, from "Four-Part Harmony"

I in the vineyard, in green-time and dead-time,
come to it dearly,
And take nature neither freaked nor amazing,
But the secret shining, the soft indeterminate wonder.

I watch it morning and noon, the unutterable sun-
downs,
And love as the leaf does the bough.

– William Everson, from "San Joaquin"

Baugi was a giant whose brother was Suttung the fiercely protective possessor of the Mead of Poetry. Baugi was also a farmer, and
so Odin, disguised as a farmhand named Bolverk, worked for Baugi
for a summer in exchange for a sip of the Mead.

It was guarded by Suttung's daughter Gunnlod, however, and
Suttung refused to offer even a drop. Odin devised a stratagem. At
his suggestion, Baugi dug into the hard mountain in which Gunnlod
sat by the Mead. Once a hole had been punched in the rock, Odin
swiftly changed himself into a snake and slithered through, much to
Baugi's chagrin at being fooled.

The three nights he spent with Gunnlod came with three
draughts of the Mead. Odin secretly spat each into a container.
When finished he changed into an eagle and flew toward Asgard.

Upon discovering this theft, Suttung changed himself into an
eagle and flew after. Watching the flight from a distance, the Aesir
laid out containers so Odin could spit in the Mead for them. Some
of it he farted out behind him, giving rise to all the bad verse of the
world. In any case, this was how the Mead of Poetry was made
available to the gods who made it available in turn to gifted poets.

They had been lavish with this gift in Fresno, where creative
miracles droop from the branches of the Tree growing in the center
of California.

I drove northward bearing along another insight learned in
Fresno about the Golden State:

People come to our coast looking for paradise, but they stay in
the Valley for a chance at redemption, hoping to turn their muck to
alchemical gold.

Merced (*solutio*)

We are the metals' first nature and only source
The highest tincture of the Art is made through us.
No fountain and no water has my like
I make both rich and poor both whole and sick.
For healthful can I be and poisonous.

—*Rosarium Philosophorum*

So far I had visited Kern, Tulare, Kings, Fresno, and now Madera, Mariposa, and Merced Counties on my journey north through the Great Central Valley. Counties grew smaller and clustered more tightly toward the top of the San Joaquin Valley and the bottom of the Sacramento above it, as though something both ecological and psychic but reducible to neither had undergone differentiation up in Gold Country. I would have to wait and see.

Madera had been developed by a lumber company, which made plain sense given that *madera* means "wood." Mariposa, "butterfly," had been a mining camp and then a logging town famous for the colorful Monarchs flying about in the spring. Mariposa County reached the foothills of the Sierras and included no incorporated cities. It bore the nickname "Mother of Counties" because twelve of them had been birthed from it.

On hot January 6, 1806, Gabriel Moraga and his men dismounted near a river and drank deeply to relieve their thirst. In gratitude Moraga named the river El Rio de la Nuestra Senora de Merced, or Merced ("Mercy") for short.

The Merced River was a tributary of another river he named, the San Joaquin, so called after the father of Mary, mother of Jesus. According to legend, Joaquin and his wife Anne had been unhappily childless for years when an angel told them to embrace in joy at the Golden Gate in Jerusalem. Making its way from the Sierras through Yosemite and down into the Valley, the San Joaquin mingles with the Sacramento at the Delta and, pouring into Suisun Bay, they flow together into the Pacific through the Golden Gate. California: where ancient tales receive geographic rebirth.

Alchemists wrote and whispered about *solutio*, the liquid aspect of the Great Work filtering, circulating, rushing, and pouring through their tubes and retorts. According to Edward Edinger, who follows Jung in psychologizing alchemy, dissolving, swimming, bathing, washing, submerging, drowning, and flooding all suggest *solutio* by which the ego is either baptized or by which it submerges into unconsciousness. Whether renewal or dissolution depends on the strength and flexibility of the conscious mind... and on the place where *solutio* occurs.

Unconsciousness: the Mariposa Indian War in 1850 between Native Californians driven off their lands and incoming miners and gold-seekers like the ruthless and scheming James D. Savage. Mining techniques of water diversion led to the Valley's first attempts at systematic irrigation.

Unconsciousness: the first Indian reservation in California between the Merced and Tuolumne Rivers, March 19, 1851.

Unconsciousness: Alabama Colony, established in 1868 near Madera, site of slaveholding Deep South cotton planters looking for a new base of operations.

Unconsciousness: Secessionists gathering at Snelling on the north bank of the Merced.

In contrast to such vulgar attempts at "whitening" emanates the immense, organic generosity of Merced, with its Great Mother mixture of mercy, dairy, dry farming, and, later, wildlife preservation. Witness tight-fisted Henry Miller, real name Heinrich Kreiser, in the 1850s, with his partner Charles Lux, grabbing 1.4 million acres of Valley land, honored by saber-rattling Otto von Bismarck in Germany, but also forgiving debts, feeding travelers, and giving grain to the destitute, meat to miners, and irrigation to local farmers. Witness educator Margaret Sheehy (1800-1865), who taught for forty-six years in Merced City, future home of a University of California campus: "Know every child, and you will love him." In the late 1800s, when almost all physicians were men, Dr. Sophia Byrd McClelland Olson of Merced helped generations of women give birth.

Merced's first administrators met informally under sheltering oaks. In those days of settlement the quality of mercy was not strained, for minor crimes in particular, all of whose committers received lenient sentences or none at all. Charles Snelling gave the county land for its first courthouse. When the railroad came to Merced in 1872, an entire block was set aside for a hotel for visitors.

Merced depended on agriculture for most of its revenue until 1941, when an Army Air Corps flying school opened in nearby Atwater, a town named after a wheat farmer. Even here, where bombers lined up for deployment in Germany and Japan, the tradition of local hospitality continued unbroken, although the red light district was closed down after the girls (who gave hot chocolate to the paperboy every day) started a clap epidemic among their Air Force patrons.

Merced's rich soil bore phenomenally well, especially potatoes, wheat, and barley, as cows lowed gently in the shade where herds of elk had once strolled by. Ceres was a town in Stanislaus County to the north, but the presence of the maternal goddess of grains and crops reached in this direction too. The Greeks knew her as Demeter, the Norse as Gerd, bright-armed wife of the harvest god Freyr.

People living close to the powers of the land know that deities personifying nature's characteristics share nature's ambivalence in full. Gerd's name refers to the earth but also means "fenced in." *Solutio* solves, but it also dissolves, disperses, and cuts apart (as the root of the word testifies). When King Erysichthon, the prototypal irresponsible logger, cut down the sacred groves of Ceres, she placed Famine in his stomach, causing him to eat all the food in the kingdom, then all the families, then his own, then himself. Henry Miller's wife died a few years after he married her, followed by his daughter Gustine, who perished in a horsing accident, followed by Henry Junior, a cripple who contracted syphilis, followed by another wife, a child, and a grandson caught in a blizzard in Oregon. Did all this tragedy have anything to do with Miller planting the original agricultural "factories in the fields" to exploit people and places alike? In Greek myth Demeter was known to keep company at times with Nemesis, terrible restorer of the balance. Is that her courthouse in the center of modern Merced?

FROM THE START OF American agriculture and settlement in the hot Valley, irrigation seemed to provide a *solution* to dryness. The very word implies a flowing around, under, over, or through obstacles to be overcome.

But if solutions work to dissolve rigidity and continue flow, then they can't be the same as fixes, explanations, or answers. "Fix" comes from "fixate," synonymous with "obsess," and *fixatio*, the operation by which a substance is pinned down into solidity or non-volatility. "Explain" means to level out, to flatten. "Answer" goes back to "reply against" and invokes a sworn statement for fixing a promise into a contract. None of these preserve the softening, penetrating fluidity of *solutio*, loose if not always fast.

Developing Merced County divided itself around the San Joaquin River, with miners on one side and ranchers on the other. Irrigation, then railroad tracks invaded its west bank; on the east this was reversed. Towns along the river disappeared as the railroad took over transport, but fields in which crops grew spread outward farther and farther. (The railroad era sounds like an event of the past, but as of 1987, the Southern Pacific Land Company still owned a hundred and fifty-three thousand acres in the San Joaquin Valley.)

The waterworks of Beale (1851 at Tejon), Miller, Lux, Easter, Church, and Boswell were only the first. By 1919, the canals and storage tanks of what would expand into the Central Valley Project, dubbed the Golden Faucet by historian Donald Worster, irrigated three million acres of private land with a volume that would reach seven million acre-feet a year, much of it pulled southward from Shasta Dam in the northern Central Valley. After being pushed along four hundred and forty-four miles of California Aqueduct, the remainder was forced nineteen hundred feet up the Tehachapi Mountains for employment on the other side.

It wasn't enough. In spite of it, agricultural pumping from aquifers still exceeds replenishment by half a trillion gallons annually while most of the revenues for crops harvested leaves the Valley, especially since the so-called Reform Act of 1982 eliminated residency requirements for growers. Case in point: Westlands Water District, the largest agricultural district in the U.S.

Even as aquifer levels fell, tainted groundwater rose in the San Joaquin Valley because of salt-laden irrigation runoff. In 1968, therefore, instead of investigating more sustainable alternatives to conserve water, the U.S. Bureau of Reclamation built a concrete channel for transporting runoff from the west side of the San Joaquin Valley into the once-pure San Joaquin River and on into the Delta. Alarms raised by downstream farmers and Bay Area environmentalists and ecologists were ignored.

Near Los Baños, where Native Californians and Mission Padres had once bathed, the initial phase of the Kesterson Reservoir and its twelve evaporation ponds were completed atop a former dairy in 1971, but only eighty-five miles of the San Luis Drain to service it was in place. Nevertheless, forty-two thousand acres of Westlands Water District cropland were hooked up to the Drain and to Kesterton, which served not only as a Reservoir but a Wildlife Refuge as well, an arrangement analogous to flushing toxic feces downstream into the water-trapping clay soils of a national park and expecting nothing bad to happen. Wildlife biologists worried about obvious dangers of exposing birds and fish to agricultural runoff were ignored as well.

In five years waves of fish die-offs and reproductive deformities grew apparent as selenium bioaccumulated, killing every fish in the evaporation ponds by 1983. That year the Delta-Mendota Canal deposited 1.6 million tons of salts: evidently the river was crying. In two years the drain and reservoir were declared toxic waste dumps and closed due to high levels of dangerous heavy metals like selenium, chromium, boron, molybdenum, and a variety of toxic salts. Ironically, Los Baños had incorporated in order to fund a sewer. A $50-million federal study was launched to figure out what had happened.

> At dawn
> Your body becomes the earth
> Licking its wounds
> Each sapling remembers
> The aches of its elders
> And each river continues
> Addressing the rocks
> Snow boils down the mountains.
>
> – Lillian Vallee, from "Los Baños Reservoir, New Melones, Etc., Etc."

After eleven years of legal action, remediation, cleanup, and new plans drawn and redrawn by the Bureau of Reclamation, the drain and reservoir were reopened. Neither had ever been completed. Westlands has offered to oversee them in exchange for guaranteed water, debt forgiveness, ownership of pumping facilities along the San Luis Canal, and lower water bills, but in spite of—or perhaps because of—backing by California Senator Dianne Feinstein, critics attempting to block a bill approving this takeover fear a powerful water monopoly.

Westland's growers have also argued that water allocation cutbacks from the Delta, where parched ecosystems are dying back and crashing, harm the westside economy because of decreased agricultural revenue. As a matter of fact, the establishment of factory-farm agriculture uniformly results in poverty. Relatively affluent whites have enjoyed the orchard-wrapped houses and schools on the county's east side since the original irrigation went on more than a century ago; west of I-99, plantations maintained by near-invisible workers stretch for thousands of acres. "Symbolically, the highway has loomed like a local version of the Berlin Wall," notes Gerald Haslam. "A place to start at bottom."

Even in wet years unemployment in Merced, Kings, Kern, and Fresno Counties often reaches 20%, with Mendota County up to 41% in 2009. By 2007, 34.6% of the residents of Huron, the largest town in the Westlands, lived below the poverty line compared to 12.4% throughout California. Fourteen percent of Huron lived 50% below the poverty line.

In the Westlands town of Mendota, "Cantaloupe Center of the World," laborers live in garages, cars, or trucks. The packing plant went under ten years ago when growers turned to migrant labor to box cantaloupes in the fields. In 2008, bankruptcy filings leaped 74% to twice the national average. By 2009, desperate men were accepting $2 per hour in wages, farmers sold uprooted almond trees for firewood, laborers stood in long lines at food banks, and virtually every block in Mendota housed illegal sheds rented out of backyards. There are no high schools in the Westlands District; but according to residents ten miles west of Mendota, there is a black-haired woman in white who passes mournfully through doors like La Llorona.

On the other hand, agribusiness revenues continue to grow, fed in part by large subsidies. According to the Environmental Working Group, Westlands farms receive $6 million in crop subsidies, $24 million in water subsidies, and $71 million in power subsidies a year, up to an average of $165,000 per farm, not counting Williamson Land Act tax breaks, technical and scientific aid, low-interest loans and grants from state agencies, and other financial advantages out of reach of low-income residents.

> In the physical and mathematical sciences, equa-
> tions defining relationships often break down at
> boundaries. I believe that similar failures occur in
> the disjunction between the social landscape of our
> suburban houses and the national and industrial
> landscapes that press against them.
>
> – Richard Meisinger

Alchemical woodcuts depict fountains (los baños) as symbols of *solutio*. In the *Rosarium Philosophorum*, or *Rose Garden of the Philosophers*, attributed to Spanish alchemist Arnold of Villanova and published in Frankfurt in 1550, the King and Queen of alchemy descend into the fountain and, now intertwined, lose their old forms and melt together. Words carved in the fountain's base describe the unity of animal, vegetable, mineral—and now human—immersed in the bath of transformation. In other manuscripts the old King enters the fountain and dissolves to make way for new interactive principles that serve rejuvenation more effectively than archaic rulership ever could.

Many fixes, explanations, and answers have been cranked out at the local, state, and federal levels to account for decades of social and ecological disaster in the agriculture-parched San Joaquin Valley, but there can be no lasting solution until the machinery of hydraulic despotism cracks enough to restore the flow of life.

ORIGINATING IN THE SIERRAS at Thousand Island Lake, the "white gold" of the San Joaquin is California's second-longest river. According to the environmental advocacy group American Rivers, it is also one of the nation's two most endangered rivers, the other being the Sacramento—the longest in California—that meets the San Joaquin at the delta. (The Colorado River is longer than either but does not originate in California.) "The Sacramento-San Joaquin Delta is on the verge of losing important fish species, and the communities that surround it already don't have adequate protection from their levees," stated director Steve Rothert. "The health of the delta depends directly on maintaining the health of these two rivers that feed it."

Friant Dam opened in the 1940s in the Sierra Nevada foothills fifteen miles north of Fresno to provide irrigation, flood control, and hydroelectric power throughout the San Joaquin Valley. Like all techno-fixes applied to complex ecosystems, it met its short-term goals at the underestimated cost of long-term consequences. Ninety-eight percent of the river that once drained more acreage than that occupied by New York and New Jersey combined no longer runs, and for sixty miles below the dam it does not run at all, going underground at Gravelly Ford in Madera County. Salmon and steelhead have nowhere to swim or spawn, and a once-thriving fishing industry has collapsed.

After eighteen years of wrangling and battling in and out of the courts, environmentalists, water users, the Department of the Interior, and the Friant Water Users Authority representing twenty-one irrigation districts agreed in 2006 on a plan for restoring water and fish below the dam while beginning the restoration of the San Joaquin River. For the Friant, setting aside water was preferable to leaving its regulation up to a judge. Also on the table: setting aside two million acres of federal lands and over a thousand miles of rivers and streams for protection from development.

In 2009, one thousand four hundred gallons per second of newly released water roared from Millerton Lake through valves opened at the base of Friant Dam. Whether enough water will circulate back from the Delta to suffice for local farming remains an open question, but after decades of human effort, salmon will now return to the river named after a future father reproached in public for his sterility. In religious iconography St. Joaquin sometimes carries a shovel.

The improved flow will also nourish the San Luis National Wildlife Refuge Complex, a forty-five-thousand-acre refuge along the river. Thirty percent of wintering birds stop here along the Pacific Flyway. Around the refuge, which oversees an additional ninety thousand acres on private lands, grows the largest region of native bunchgrass and wetlands left in California after the Central Valley Project drained 95% of the Valley's wetlands. Here in the wide lap of Ceres thrive ducks, herons, egrets, hawks, owls, song-birds, plovers, cranes, frogs, crayfish, turtles, and a number of at-risk species, including the horned lark, the tiger salamander, the vernal tadpole shrimp, the Aleutian Canada goose, the tri-colored blackbird, the kit fox, and the white-faced ibis. On former ranch-land volunteers and employees from Ducks Unlimited, the National Audubon Society, the North American Wetland Conservation grant program, and the Bureau of Reclamation have worked to undo the damage of unsustainable agriculture and rebuild the wetlands and their profusion of welcoming habitats.

A common argument leveled against such efforts to conserve and repair is that setting aside land and water for wilderness is bad for business. Thanks to money granted from the Fish and Wildlife Service to the refuge, a new headquarters building and visitor center will bring business into nearby Los Baños. Visitors to the refuge will stay overnight in town, eat at local restaurants, and shop at local retailers. They will also receive an education on the impor-tance of preserving wetlands. The center will be housed in a build-ing designed to generate more energy than it uses. One big window will look out onto grazing tule elk.

As for the Merced River, it too has seen its share of woes. In 1936 six dredges tore up its bottom in search of gold; they stopped oper-ating in 1952, but cultivation of arable land around the river spread until four thousand sets of control gates and seven hundred and ninety-three miles of canals sucked away water to irrigate over a hundred and fifty-four thousand acres of cropland. Runoff return-ing to the river carries pesticides, nitrates, and other contaminates. Even so, the river's generosity extends to keeping the San Joaquin River going below their confluence near Turlock. Above the conflu-ence the river trickles out.

Federal licenses for three of the Merced's four dams are up for renewal, giving groups like Friends of the River an opportunity to renegotiate water release and distribution in accord with updated ecological standards. Other goals for restoration include planting riparian vegetation, alfalfa crops to provide wildlife habitat, cleanup of mine tailings left in the floodplain, curbing of housing and industrial sprawl, accumulation of spawning gravel for salmon, wildlife buffers and zoning, and habitat repair to foster biodiversity. Increased water alone would relieve at least some of Mother Merced's decades-long weariness. At present a hatchery below the Merced's lowest dam allow chinook salmon to swim up a fish ladder into spawning pools.

In *Aion* Jung writes about the fish as a symbol of cyclical renewal and rebirth (baptismal baths were nicknamed "fish ponds" long ago), of redemption (as in the figure of Christ and his "fishers of men"), of spiritual food to be eaten ceremonially, of a numinous Self image swimming in the unconscious, and of a mobile incarnation of the soul. To fish with respect and skill is to catch and assimilate psychological, cultural, and spiritual nourishment. To find a fish means to receive the gift of a new truth, as when a jewel or ring pops out of the fish's mouth.

In alchemy the fish symbolizes both Prime Matter and Philosopher's Stone as it swims about in the alchemical fountain. Glowing fish eyes shine forth the sparks of the World Soul awakening in the bath as emblems of non-human nature in possession of its own kind of consciousness. (From where else do we suppose we got ours?)

My Irish ancestors told tales of how eating the Salmon of Knowledge brought wisdom and second sight. The Welsh who came before me also linked this fish to knowledge; one immense salmon even gave an early version of King Arthur a ride on its back. In Norse myth the trickster Loki changed his shape into that of a salmon to escape divine retribution. The English word "salmon" might derive from a root that means "flow."

Here in California, the Miwoks spoke of how when evil spirits locked up all the salmon, smooth-tongued Coyote talked the spirits into giving him the key, which he promptly used to release their captives. In the creation stories of the Pacific Northwest, salmon were provided by the gods to feed and look after human beings. Salmon were of such importance that the word for them means "food" and "eat" in some Native Californian languages: "I'm hungry, let's go salmon lunch." The presence of salmon allowed permanent

residence along rivers and streams, gave structure to cyclical ceremonies, offered a connection to the sacred, bestowed wisdom, prosperity, and luck. None were caught until enough passed upstream
to assure future abundance.

Because salmon are anadromous, swimming thousands of miles
for several years in the sea before returning to the freshwater rivers
of their birth to spawn, they recollect in their movements and the
songs and dances that celebrate them the great cycles that hold land
and water together. Bringing nitrogen from the sea to the earth
through the animals that eat them, salmon remain partners of
renewal. When the salmon cycle is interrupted, renewal cannot
take place, outwardly or inwardly, and the long-sought arrival their
travels signify cannot punctuate an extended exile.

Salmon: soul with fins. What will it take to let them (and us?)
finally come home? Little more than water and good habitat. Earth
looks after the rest, as always.

If how we treat rivers reflects our comfort with the flow of life,
if *solutio* fixated, redirected, dammed, or backed up implies similar
diminishment of community and vitality, then giving back to
watery beings from whose lateral depths we have taken so much
restores us to ourselves and to each other.

Modesto (*circulatio*)

When I've spoken to Valley people about what it's like to live in the belly of California, sooner or later, especially in those who were born here, a certain modesty is liable to surface. Not always. But when it appears, it feels like a half-acknowledged but resigned unwillingness to stand out too much or aim too high.

We are used to thinking about such habits of mind as personal or cultural, but might this one be geographic as well? The city of Taft was once named Moro, but an official of the Southern Pacific did not want the name confused with that of Morro Bay and changed it to Moron. Maricopa changed to high-sounding Monarch in 1907, but changed back again. Fresno took its name from *Fraxinus oregona*, a small tree nobody could find because it hid up in the foothills.

This diffidence seems to intensify in the upper half of the San Joaquin Valley, a region about which Delores Cabezut-Ortiz wrote an apologetic Preface to her book *Merced County: The Golden Harvest*. In Jeanette Maino's preface to *One Hundred Years....Modesto, California 1870-1970*, she too apologized: "...We are all aware that there will be mistakes. We hope none have been caused by carelessness. Five people witnessing an accident will have five different versions of it, and in assembling our account of Modesto's 100 years, we have encountered all five." In his book on Modesto B.G. Osborn went so far as to handwrite this in the copy I obtained in the city historical museum: "This is not about me and my photograph should not be on the cover." (The cover refers to "A B.J. Osborn History.") "We can now print, bind and ship a niche book like this one—one book at a time. But error can still creep in. Sorry about the book's cover, and I hope you not judge it by the cover. What you pay for this book is my contribution to the museum." So be it.

The Old Fisherman's Club that met in a shack on a ranch near Patterson went without a name for five years after its founding. The Gallo winery is still an anonymous building. Nearby Denair was Elmwood, then Elmdale, then Elms, then back to Elmwood before settling on Denair, the name of a local landowner. Clyde changed to Thalheim, and then to Valley Home (the literal meaning of *thalheim*) as anti-German sentiment swept the county during World War I. Islip's Ferry was known as Burney's, Warren's, Hughes', Keyes', and Walker's Ferry. The Stanislaus River was called, at one time or another, Rio de Nuestra Senora de Guadalupe, Rio Laquisimes, Appelaminy, Smith's River, Rio de Estanislao, and John Fremont's anglicized current version.

Some nearby towns were so modest that they faded away without even a civic identity crisis left behind. New Hope, Adamsville, and Tuolumne City disappeared, as did San Joaquin City (founded by Charles Imus to capture and sell wild horses), Stanislaus City, Turner's Ferry, Hills Ferry, South Tuolumne Landing, Bell's Landing, Patterson's Landing, Mahoney's Landing, Orestimba, Mercedes City, Hill's Ferry, Berryville, Burneyville, Byersville, Langworth, Twenty-Six Mile House, Twenty-Eight Mile House, Adamsville, Westport, Paradise City, Crescent City, Empire City, Patricksville, La Grange, Grayson (founded by Missouri plantation owner Andrew Jackson Grayson), and Crows Landing (now unincorporated, and with toxins detected nearby).

Modesto was to be named after railroad tycoon William Ralston, founder of the Bank of California, but he refused, for which he was called "muy modesto." Judge Archibald Stakes then decided, "The parent of the infant is Modesty—then the baby's name must be

Modesto." Ralston's body was found floating in San Francisco Bay after a run on his bank, but the place named after him lived on.

I headed for it up 99, noting scattered, dissociated sights going by: clumps of brush and patches of dry grass, a camper shell too small for its pickup truck, a blue bend of aqueduct, high green orchards next to barren fields... In Turlock, old houses stacked beside each other like headstones in the cemetery and shops in the sprawling strip mall to the north... A peeling billboard of singers wearing cowboy hats... "Nobody Takes Care of You Like State Farm. Nobody." *Including State Farm.* In Manteca, a town a little south of Modesto, a billboard blared, "Life, Money, Hope" at the freeway from the Crossroads Grace Church.

Miles of empty railroad cars, many disfigured with graffiti... a field of dirt... wooden power poles like lonely crosses, bearing amperage instead of grace... on a trucker's mudflap, a steer head perched above a cross... the dry Fresno River... crop rows, wires, roads, fences, dividers, tracks, cars, trains, all in blocks and lines running straight across and through...

Before this trip I had spent an hour listening to Joan, a colleague, talk about growing up in Turlock. I had asked her first about growing up in the Valley, but she replied that "Valley people" don't see themselves as Valley people so much as coming from specific places in the Valley. But the further south they came from, the lower in the unspoken Valley social strata. Mexicans lived west of the train tracks in many of the towns.

Then as now, Turlock (from *tuar lach*, Irish for "dry place," so named after settler John Mitchell declined to have a town named after himself) was ethnically diverse four decades ago, with Swedes, Japanese, Chinese, Portuguese from the Azores, Assyrians, Sikhs, and Mexicans all mixing as children at play but not much as adults. Residents grew walnuts, almonds, and peaches in the sandy soil. Life revolved around major crops but mechanically, as when school children got "the call" via telephone to leave class to go into the fields and turn on the irrigation. Sometimes hoofed animals made pets, but more often livestock and livelihood. The Great Depression had taught unremitting frugality: everything was saved, cans, string, garments, paper, everything.

Frugality went with an iron stoicism and intense religious conservatism (there were many churches in town). Embarrassing one's family earned one a ticket straight to Hell and ostracism, as did "making waves" in the landlocked Valley. On the other hand, people could be helpful, guardedly friendly, and very giving, pulling together with little discussion when things fell apart.

Tidy front lawns led onto a flat world where anyone with a car could just drive and drive, going anywhere, but only in two dimensions. Flatness and straightness and lines felt safe, but San Francisco (for example) was disconcerting because one could get lost going up or down there.

For the young this Euclidean limbo meant deep boredom. Teens cruised in circles, passing the time in the hope that something would happen. Endless waiting for nobody knew what. Summers brought such immobilizing heat that everything slowed or stopped; kids fled sweating to the canals to chat, smoke, neck, or drink beer until the evening warmth dropped down to tolerable. One could see the stars until the winter fogs rolled in, deadening everything; only in spring did the land and its occupants rise fully to life, starting in February when crops and orchards bloomed.

What had changed in Turlock over the decades? Cal State Stanislaus had come to town, as had housing developments and big retail stores (I had seen them lining 99 with their standardized sameness).

I spent an afternoon leafing through the yellowed pages of old newspapers Joan had inherited. Impressions:

On the masthead, a Walt Disney cartoon of a giant grinning bee hoisting a waving American flag. The caption informed me that his name was Scoopy.

From the front page of the *Modesto Bee*, July 3, 1970:

STATE GETS AID FOR ANTICRIME TASK FORCE

"...to set up a highly specialized task force to combat organized crime."

RUSS-MIDEAST STIRS NEW U.S. WORRIES

"The Nixon administration is now convinced that Soviet air combat forces must be expelled from Egypt, through negotiations if possible, before they can become a springboard for long-term Soviet domination of the Mediterranean and the Middle East."

REDS SHIFT BIG UNIT TO CAMBODIA

"...In the face of the North Vietnamese attacks, which the official said the Cambodians considered an invasion, volunteers were flocking into military duty."

Already I could see the slant. I read on:

NIXON SENDS CONGRATULATIONS

"Never before have the contributions of your community been so vital to the progress and welfare of your country." Ronald McDonald's congratulations appeared on page C-12. "Watch for Ronald in Tomorrow's Parade! Free Gifts for All the Kiddies!"

COWBOY MARSHAL

"Ed Mape, west Modesto rancher, will lead Modesto's Centennial Fourth of July parade tomorrow as grand marshal of the 200-plus entry event."

The yellowing sheet crackled as it turned. Page 2:

TEALE LEADS FIGHT AS SENATE AGAIN TURNS DOWN BUDGET

REAGAN STANDS PAT ON BUDGET

WORKERS WAIT WITHOUT VISIBLE PAYDAY ALARM

Hard to believe.

BOTH PARTIES WANT TO PUT AN END TO CRISES

Harder still.

The back page displayed two large photographs of the Statue of Liberty separated by a quotation: "I LIFT UP MY LAMP BESIDE THE GOLDEN DOOR!" I wonder what the farmworkers of 1970 would have thought about these fine words. Or the farmworkers of today...

From the "City News in Brief" section I learned that a trial was scheduled for one Joe Dale Furr of Modesto for two counts of check fraud and three counts of forgery; that at DePonte's, a Sheet Metal Journeyman would also work on air conditioning; that Lonnie Thomas Browning of Empire pleaded innocent by reason of insanity to two counts of assault on peace officers; and that "Prayer Accomplishes miracles. For personal—loving help call Chapel of Prayer...." They needed loving help with their grammar. Even by 1970, I could see, local news had shrunk to the status of a wrapper around ads for fast food, General Motors, and Montgomery Ward.

Scattered headlines from the *Bee* that year:

FARMERS ABANDONED WHEAT AFTER THE CANALS WERE FILLED

A GLORIOUS FOURTH WAS ENJOYED BY ALL

EDITOR'S GUN WENT OFF IN HIS POCKET

CITY ENACTS AUTO LAW (official speed limit 15 mph)

ANTI-IRRIGATION FORCES FOUGHT A STUBBORN BATTLE

SCORNED CHINESE LEFT THEIR MARK

CITY FOUGHT FIRE WITH WATER, PRAYER

RAIL VENDETTA BECOMES A BLOOD BATH

Below this story:

Are you looking for beer

   Your poor heart to cheer?

Then to Jacobsen's, go quick!

   He keeps it on ice,

It tastes awful nice;

   To your ribs it ever will stick.

Not much of a substitute, Jacobsen's beer, alas, for the Mead of Poetry that had ended up in Fresno.

HERE IN THE LANDS of the Laquisimas Yokuts, John James Atherton paid $1,800 for a hundred and sixty acres. A year later the Contract and Finance Company owned by Crocker of the Central Pacific bought him out. The tracks arrived in November, and, beginning with a saloon, the town built itself up around the station. Bridges, fords, and ferries followed because Stanislaus County, separated from Tuolumne County in 1854, was crisscrossed by rivers and streams. Wheat ranches spread, as did ditches and canals, with Ceres the first U.S. town to receive water from publicly owned irrigation (1909).

By 1911, local businessmen were thinking up schemes for luring people to Modesto to promote economic growth. Boosters and realtors rode around on railroad cars converted into showrooms of displays of Modesto's crops, handed out brochures on Market Street in San Francisco, and erected screens in the Ferry Building there to project images of the agricultural abundance. Signs posted outside the building asked passersby why people should settle in Stanislaus County and answered with evocations of sunlight and water, foothills and plains, orange groves and even olive oil fountains.

A contest was held in 1912 to select a slogan for a French Renaissance arch to be designed by Bernard Joseph and placed at Ninth and I Streets to welcome visitors to Modesto. The winning slogan, an aimless and rather defensive boast—"Nobody's Got Modesto's Goat"—was rejected finally in favor of "Water, Wealth, Contentment, Health":

> O, Stanislaus is a paradise
> Which no one can deny
> Look for Water, Wealth, Contentment, Health
> And never pass it by.

The arch contained six hundred and thirty incandescent bulbs and was posted on stands of solid concrete. With detectable envy the *Turlock Tribune* snubbed it as "too cheap for Turlock."

With the arch came a song, "Modesto, Where Dreams Come True," courtesy of Winifred McGee, made the official song of Modesto by Resolution 881 adopted April 9, 1924:

> There's just one spot in the world for me
> No matter where I roam.
> A wonderful city, most fair to see,
> Modesto is my home.
> With golden beauty upon its fields,
> Its flowers of every hue,
> Its towers of learning,
> Its homes so blest,
> Modesto, I love you.

CHORUS:

> My Modesto where dreams come true
> We'll be loyal and true to you,
> City of water, City of wealth,
> City of contentment, City of health,
> Fairest and blest of the great Golden West,
> Modesty, the city of my dreams.
> Our founders brave in days gone by
> Together toiled and planned;
> So we will keep our courage high;

Together we will stand.
With high endeavor we'll work for this,
The city of the west.
We're here to serve,
And here to build.
Modesto, we pledge our best.

Three fashion shows and a parade of marchers, eighty-five automobiles, and twenty motorcycles launched the March 1912 arch dedication. Acting Mayor George Perley's speech at the base of the arch was drowned by the roar of engines.

In photographs I snapped after reading the arch's plaque, a McDonald's crouched on the corner of Ninth and I. I wondered in passing how Modestans felt about being greeted by Ronald. On the way into town I had seen new housing developments topped with red tile roofs crowding out green cropland. The boosters has succeeded beyond all expectations, but the ever-fluctuating economy, further destabilized by hedge funds, risky real estate loans, energy speculation, tax cuts for the wealthy, and perpetual war, turned their victory into a hollow one. Already new neighborhoods stood vacant and silent, the strip malls servicing them filled with FOR RENT signs on empty windows, in hard-hit cities like Tracy and Stockton.

Kathryn, my traveling companion for this trip, would accompany me into Gold Country once we reached the Sacramento Valley north of here, territory she knew far better than I. She was along to see how I worked with Californian places. Her depth psychology training and natural intuition made her a quick study, and her willingness to drive left me free to take notes.

Walking by a Pentacostal "Revival Center" (quotation marks included on its sign for reasons unknown), we passed beneath the arch again and walked down town, pausing at length in front of a clock made of flowers. At twenty feet in diameter it included twenty-five thousand blossoms planted by the Modesto Garden Club twice a year. Above feverfew daisies, violas, pansies, and begonias the clock hand moved incrementally. A fat man in a round hat pulled out a gold pocket watch and announced to no one in particular, "12:30. Not bad for 1913."

We were in a town of circular designs, we could see, including the old railroad roundhouse and the fountain on the grounds of the Stanislaus County Courthouse. At one time almost every residence had a windmill, as did the courthouse roof. (After we left, wayfaring monks from the relocated Drepung Loseling Monastery would draw a ceremonial mandala for the Modesto Junior College art gallery.)

In the fountain stood a bronze likeness of Chief Estanislao raising his right palm as though to stop the traffic. I nodded and began to chuckle, raising my camera.

"You already know what's here?" Kathryn asked me. I nodded again and explained.

Estanislao was the Spanish name of Cucunuchi, a Yokuts leader born near here on a bank of the Stanislaus River. ("Estanislao" means "glory of his camp" or "village.") He entered Mission San Jose in Alameda County to the west as an acolyte, but he emerged a guerrilla raider who led as many as four thousand followers against the missions and their outposts. He had learned military tactics at the mission. Remarkably, his attacks resulted in much booty but few casualties.

This changed, however, in 1829, when General Mariano Vallejo took the field against him with a larger force. Estanislao survived and was pardoned, but in three years he was raiding again. Some of his outriders wore masks.

Pacification expeditions and diseases took a heavy toll on the Yokuts and other Indian populations as more and more settlers moved into California. Eventually Estanislao ended up at Mission San Jose again, this time as an instructor of native languages. He might have died in a cholera outbreak in 1833.

Despite its modest name, this place seemed to attract rebellion. In fact, the town incorporated in part to present a unified force against rampant crime and lawlessness, some of which centered on the crooked lawyers stationed down aptly named Front Street. James "Grizzly" Adams, renegade and loner, had helped extinguish the California grizzly here, and fur trappers hunted here illegally. As early as 1879, a band calling itself the San Joaquin Valley Regulars, men who rounded up hookers and gamblers and put them on the morning train out of town, turned vigilante and became outlaws themselves. The gunslinger Joaquin Murietta had been no stranger here either. The town marshal played poker in dives, and the trustees were often drunk.

Drama productions told the rebel tale from the first ever staged in town: *Ten Nights in a Bar Room*. The Modesto Theater opened in February of 1913 with a performance of *Pirates of Penzance*; the Strand opened in 1921 with *Mark of Zorro*. Famous Modestans include the rebellious "Pappy" Boyington, Jack Palance, Sam Peckinpah of *The Wild Bunch* fame, and George Lucas, who based his own film "*American Graffiti*" on conflicts between conformity and rebellion witnessed here before he left the Valley. The boredom of Luke Skywalker echoes the boredom of Lucas stranded among farmers with nothing to do but cruise.

Is it any wonder that the statue of Justice atop the county courthouse lost her scales, keeping only her sword? I chuckled again to see an ad for GLADIATOR - LOW-COST AUTO INSURANCE, and another for an Anarchist Cafe at Tenth and J.

Someone here had noticed the shadow of the rebel, judging from other signs downtown:

CRUISING PROHIBITED

LOITERING PROHIBITED

CURFEW

THIS SITE UNDER VIDEO SURVEILLANCE

Police patrols searched for vandals who destroyed eighty headstones in two cemeteries.

The rebel motif reminded me of coastal San Benito County's, but with a difference. The county named after St. Benedict actually held the energy of the permanent outlaw—like the Hells Angels who make their two-wheeled pilgrimage to Hollister year after year. Underneath the nonconformist persona the *rebel* (from *bellum*, "war") involves a very different psychology from that of the outlaw. As novelist Frank Herbert noted cynically but with some accuracy, the rebel often turns out to be a closet aristocrat. Rebels engage in revolution, the root of which is "revolve." "Meet the new boss, same as the old boss." Revolution: a faithful mechanism for converting rebels into rulers who then fight off the outlaws. (Some would object to this characterization by pointing to the apparent success of the American Revolution, but as historian Howard Zinn has shown, the colonial elite never ceded power. Its real genius shone in its efficiency at converting peasants and farmers into soldiery. The ruling class of attorneys and wealthy landowners took the place of the British and kept it. A change of ownership is not a revolution.)

In Modesto we noticed lots of groups of boys. Five of them, three wearing hats, slouched in the Denny's parking lot with Knight's Inn behind them. From Five Points I made a counterclockwise pivot to observe: the Denny's, a small strip mall (Home Theater, Aames, a palm reader, USA Nails and Hair, Computer Express), Giarelli Associates, Jack-in-the-Box, and finally Lucas Plaza, with a statue of boy and girl and car. The State Theater stood next door to Queen Mab's, named consciously or unconsciously after the powerful Celtic goddess who tried to tame rebellious Cuchulainn.

The NO CRUISING signs felt out of place in a city where George Lucas had nearly died in a car accident before leaving the Valley as a renegade filmmaker destined to cruise mainstream. Not long after its founding, Modesto itself had been hoisted up on wheels and moved away from the river and toward the railroad.

Down the decades the Modestan love of circular motion (the "revolve" in "revolution"?) underwent many upgrades but never changed its basic direction. Driving twenty-mule and -horse teams through town once constituted a local sport, but by 1893, a memorial fountain built for citizen Simpson Rogers slowed traffic by snagging wagon wheels; a bicycle craze seized the city a year later. 1909 saw President Taft starting a speech when his train left the station prematurely. When it returned, he went on, "As I was saying the last time I was here..." In 1913, the year the Panama-Pacific Road Race passed through Modesto, "Automobile Gateway to Yosemite," less formal car races roared down Seventh between I and G. To circumvent a car noise law, drivers installed a muffler bypass operated by a foot pedal. For an auto parade for Civil War vets, cars carried decorations and names of soldiers. In the sinister year of 1923, when the Ku Klux Klan held "classes" for new members a few miles out of town, two thousand cars parked around the altar. As another war loomed and the Great Depression worsened, Modesto spent twice as much per capita on cars than on food. "Migrant Mother" Dorothy Thompson managed a trailer court and drove around town in an old Cadillac. In September of 1934, "Night Rider" motorists with license plates removed from their cars told Filipinos to leave the county. By 1947 prospective drivers had to be on a six-month waiting list to buy cars. When the A&W Drive-In opened in 1957, the car hops all wore roller skates.

Alchemically, this imagery recalls the operation of *circulatio:* fluid refined by spinning it through loops and curls of tubing. Understood psychologically, *circulatio* brings back old stories of wounding repeated over and over to provide fresh chances at resolution. Freud had named this "repetition compulsion" but misunderstood it as mere self-defeat. He would not have comprehended why George Lucas and his young compadres had driven in circles around downtown Modesto at night on the lookout for new twists in the same old story.

Freud had been correct, however, in observing the deadliness of *circulatio* spun out unconsciously. On Yosemite Boulevard just north of the airport we saw six sorrowful teens seated near a makeshift street altar. Three were weeping. A fifty-year-old woman named Alma had just been fatally struck here by two cars. The first fled the scene. The second, a blue van, had also injured a bystander who tried to intervene on the woman's behalf. It had been raining, the mourners explained to us, and Alma, who was deaf, had tried to cross the busy street.

"ALMA REED" read a strip of cardboard stuck up on a Salvation Army sign; "rest in peace....you may be gone but never forgotten." Someone had scrawled for her a turtle wearing a cap. It occurred to me then that *alma* meant "soul," the first precious sacrifice to the cultural cult of speed.

LIKE REBELLION, CONSERVATISM, WHICH in extreme cases constitutes a rebellion against Time itself, has a way of strengthening what it would repress. Ralph Taylor, executive secretary of the Agricultural Council of California, demonstrated this in 1938 by denouncing *The Grapes of Wrath*. He objected, he stated, to its "filth and profanity," but not to the inhuman labor conditions and dreadful misery that had prompted the novel. Its popularity increased still more once the city banned it from schools and libraries. In a blind *circulatio* of the same futile logic of repression, the county ordered its Japanese American citizens to register in Modesto at the Winter Garden in 1942 before gathering in Turlock to be deported. The Japanese are still here. In 1953, the city's School Board refused to reinstate a Modesto High instructor for mentioning the world's major religions in his Pacific History course. Naturally, this fostered intense curiosity about non-Christian faiths.

Likewise, respectable Modesto citizens have struggled against alcohol production and consumption since the city's founding around a train station saloon. By the 1880s, the Ancient Order of Druids ran the Stanislaus Brewery, and by 1908, Wood Colony called its congregation "Drunkards." Many decades later, churchgoing locals still pushed hard for abstinence and, eventually, for Prohibition (1920-1933), when speakeasies called "blind pigs" ran amok and a large alcohol factory operated in town; but in the end, the thoroughly unscrupulous Gallo Brothers dominated Modesto and still do.

"Gallos" should not be confused with "gallows," although the first man sentenced to execution in the county was hung in Stockton because Modesto lacked the proper equipment. By contrast, *gallo* is Italian for "rooster." It is also a family name that Ernest and Julio Gallo sued their younger brother Joseph for using. This was in 1986, when Joseph sold cheese. He countered with the claim that the brothers owed him a third of their winery because they had launched it with his inheritance. When the gavel had crowed three times, wielded by a judge with undisclosed conflicts of interest, Joseph lost and was forced to change the name of his dairy and cheese business to "Joseph Farms." Ernest would also initiate lawsuits against business owners unrelated to him but legitimately named "Gallo" to get their name off their products. He believed he owned it.

This detail is important for understanding the tactics resorted to by Gallo to dominate Californian wine production. Ninety percent of all American wine ships from California. The top twenty wineries, including Constellation, Beringer, Kendall-Jackson, Yellow Tail, Woodbridge, Franzia, and Gallo, control 80% of that wine under various labels, and the top fifty wineries nearly 95% of it. Since the early 1980s, large companies have invested in wine: companies like Heublein (owners of KFC and Smirnov), Seagram, Coca-Cola Company, Pillsbury, Nestle, and RJR Nabisco. Middlemen arranged in distribution monopolies going back to the days of Al Capone profit immensely because of regulations that make shipping wine a felony in some states. Here again a ban only encourages illicit profit.

> I believe wine is an extension of the winemaker's personality.
>
> —Mike Martini.

The Gallo family entered the wine trade as bootleggers during the Depression years (1929 until World War II), a fact contradicting Ernest and Julio's modest claims of having taught themselves winemaking from a pamphlet in the library. Nor did they start with only $5,900 to their name. Before the bootlegging, Joe Gallo, their father, had stenciled "GALLO" on wine barrels in Oakland as early as 1906.

By many accounts Joe Senior was a violent drunk who beat his wife and children except for Joseph Junior, the favorite. The older brothers ran away when he pointed a shotgun at their mother but returned when he calmed down. His brother Mike was confined San Quentin and other prisons. Joe Senior brought his family to

Modesto in 1924 and put them to work in the fields. (Joan knew
Ernest and Julio and remembered seeing them falling asleep at
school from exhaustion.)

When the boys got older, Joe Senior sent them on trips to
Chicago, not as full partners in the wine business, which they never
were, but as agents of it. According to author Jerome Tuccille, they
worked directly with Al Capone, and Julio also worked with the
New York mob. Ernest bragged later about having dealt with
Scarface in person.

By 1932, Joe Senior and his wife had moved into a shabby house
in Fresno, as though hiding from someone. They had no phone or
electricity. Ernest and Julio were left mysteriously in charge of the
Modesto vineyards and shipping business. Prohibition was in effect,
so the grapes were ostensibly for non-alcoholic use and the occasional church Communion. Ernest claimed later to have tried to talk
his reluctant father into starting an actual winery, having foreseen
that Prohibition would lift in 1933, but (it later emerged) Joe Senior
already owned a large supply of grapes and a set of underground
storage tanks: in other words, a winery a few steps from becoming
fully operational. In June of 1933, Ernest's application to open a
bonded wine storeroom was denied by the Prohibition Office in San
Francisco on the grounds that he did not own a winery.

On the day this took place, Joe Junior saw (he related later) a
heated argument between his father and Julio at the Fresno ranch.
Julio told Joe Junior to drive his mother and Aileen, Julio's new wife,
around the ranch while the conversation continued. According to
Joe Junior, his mother's last words when he returned were, "I don't
care what happens to me. All I want is for you boys to work together and get along." To Joe she said, "Be good, and mind your brothers." One day later, she and Joe Senior were found shot to death in
an apparent murder-suicide.

Ernest blamed this tragedy on his father's poor health and
"financial reverses," but Joe Senior's bank accounts were far from
empty. A recent loan of $31,000 dollars was missing, however. No
suicide note was recovered. The gun was found near Joe Senior's
hand instead of in it. His fingerprints were on the barrel but not on

the handle. Why hadn't he fallen with gun in hand? Why did a bottle of wine in the kitchen bear Joe's fingerprints when no glasses stood nearby? Why had Joe and Aileen arrived on the day before the shooting to pick up Joe Junior ahead of previous arrangements? Why had the dogs been shot as well? The mailbox on the ranch held an envelope containing payment for the couple's property taxes. Why would a man contemplating suicide and murder pay the bills? No one followed up these anomalies.

Later speculation would introduce the specter of a mob hit inflicted after Joe Senior borrowed money from the wrong people. If so, was it a coincidence that the murder weapon, a Smith & Wesson .32, was the same model Ernest had purchased in 1930 in Chicago and later claimed to have misplaced? And why would Joe Senior need to borrow if he had money in the bank? Joe Junior's version of events, later recited in court when his brothers sued him, certainly made it sound like his father and mother knew they would be killed. And what about the argument between Julio and Joe Senior going on a day after Ernest's rejected application? Journalist Ellen Hawkes's book *Blood & Wine* begins with a haunting quotation by Balzac: "The secret of great fortunes with no apparent source is a forgotten crime, forgotten because it was properly carried out."

With Joe Senior dead and Prohibition ended, Ernest and Julio proceeded to set up their winery. Joe Junior was thirteen, and the will set his inheritance at a third of the family estate. A key point in the future lawsuit would hinge on whether he knowingly signed his inheritance over to Ernest and Julio. Like the biblical Joseph of the coat of many colors, he, the former favorite of his father, would claim that his brothers sold him out.

Henry Ford had turned car-making into a production line, and Ray Kroc the same with McDonald's hamburgers. Ernest and Julio now applied this mechanistic practice to winemaking. As they did they made additional revenue by scraping cream of tartar from their wine tanks for wartime explosives, selling grain alcohol nicknamed "torpedo juice" for patrol boat motors, and converting molasses into an alcohol used by the military for synthetic rubber. The Gallos used this government money to expand the business. Nonetheless, the winery found itself on probation and fined for illegally coloring its brandy.

All in all the Gallo brothers had a busy war. Joe was turned down for the Coast Guard for being colorblind, but the U.S. Army accepted him and he went on to win several medals of valor. Taking advantage of wartime price controls that held grape sales down, Ernest went around to growers in California and signed them up for higher profits for next season. When the controls were lifted, Gallo found itself in control of 75% of the state's grapes and able to sell them at enormous profits due to the artificial scarcity.

Ernest had been nicknamed "the Lawyer" by his father for good reason. While keeping an eye on the competition (marrying Amelia Franzia to obtain her family's winery when he failed to put them out of business), the other eye noticed one Charles Gallo, whom he sued for a name infringement. Ernest won, and Charles Gallo, now ruined financially, died of a heart attack.

Ernest was learning the value of catchy marketing. The October 1945 issue of *Life* had featured the "Queen of the Crush," a young soda clerk emerging from a vat of Gallo wine. (Ernest put her on the payroll temporarily to avoid the accusation of having exploited her.) As the pipe-extruding winery began to resemble an oil refinery, it cranked out screw caps, cardboard ads around bottle necks, and the bottles themselves. Promotional material went up on billboards along highways and into grocery and liquor stores, where Gallo salesmen did occasional rearranging to put Gallo wares in front of competing merchandise. Somehow that merchandise often disappeared or was found with punctured caps and corks, or smeared with coats of oil that collected dust. Regional Gallo managers enforced a conservative dress code—clean-shaven, no beards—and noted down employees' personal problems for later reference. Gallo spies infiltrated distributorships and competing wineries.

Ernest went to Capone associate Mike Romano for help marketing Gallo in Chicago. After a rough start the wine was duly distributed.

Gallo's methods enabled it to mass-produce relatively cheap and moderately sweet wine that proved extremely popular over many decades. Andre (1966) tasted like soda pop, and Boone's Farm Apple Wine like cider. Bartles & Jaymes announced the wine cooler in 1981; Ripple (early 1950s) was even carbonated. This campaign reached a new high—or low—in Thunderbird, bottled in 1957, named after Ford's 1954 sports car because of its powerful kick, and announced by Princess Thunderbird, a model in a tight Indian out-fit. Marketers targeted not only Native Americans in the southwest, but ghettos and other poor areas, especially in Los Angeles, Houston, Shreveport, New York City, and Modesto, where taste tests had to be discontinued because African Americans specifical-ly solicited for them left the winery drunk. Empty bottles appearing in gutters increased product visibility. According to one account, Ernest and his ad man Fenderson were stopped at an intersection in an Atlanta slum when Ernest called out from the car to a wino on the sidewalk, "What's the word?" "Thunderbird," the man answered, completing the Gallo jingle to Ernest's keen delight.

Cheap wines brought revenue, but they also spread Gallo's rep-utation as a manufacturer of rotgut. To counter this perception, Gallo removed its name from Thunderbird labels but kept selling "ghetto blasters": fortified wines so dubbed by their salesmen. On the other hand, the Cherokee brand never did well; the ersatz Sioux in full headdress on the label didn't help. "Ernest seemed to believe that what we really needed to do," said a top Gallo employee, "was to change people's perceptions instead of upgrading the products. In reality, he was afraid that a boost in quality would hurt his mar-ket share." Charlie, a Gallo employee and cousin of Ernest's wife, was renamed Carlo Rossi and presented to the public as an old Italian winemaker. This worked well enough that "Rossi" was asked for autographs. In parades through the Central Valley he sat on floats, dressed in overalls and sipping wine.

In some respects life in the Gallo home, a redwood ranch on Maze Road with a street number but no name, recalled the darkness and secrecy of the Joe Senior days. Ernest, a drinker, spent all morn-ing wine-tasting while his wife shopped compulsively. Julio's son Philip was subjected to a series of "cures" for the homosexuality nobody discussed and killed himself with a shotgun blast. He was

buried near his grandparents. Ernest's son David would die mysteriously in a bathtub. In 1967, Joe Junior left to concentrate on dairy
ranching and grape-growing.

The grape boycott led by Cesar Chavez in 1973 hurt sales for a
time, especially when Gallo sided with the Teamsters against the
United Farm Workers and tried to have strikers evicted from their
homes. Class action lawsuits claimed that Gallo fooled consumers
by removing its name from various brands (including Franzia's
"Two-Buck Chuck"). When independent distributors complained
about pressure from Gallo, the Federal Trade Commission began an
investigation that prompted much shredding and burning of files.
But from 1972, winemaking boomed in California thanks to a self-
fulfilling Bank of America prediction that wine production and consumption would swell rapidly. Buying and giving the McHenry
Mansion to Modesto, investing in a new medical education building
there, constructing a Gallo Center for the Arts modeled after the
Roman Colosseum, funding viticulture and oenology programs at
Fresno State, U.C. Davis, and Stanford Medical School: these and
other ostensibly charitable acts improved Gallo's image, at least in
California. In 1978 Senator Alan Cranston pushed through an
amendment to ensure that tax breaks granted to family corporations applied to big ones too; insiders nicknamed this the Gallo
Wine Amendment. Gallo thanked him by contributing to his reelec-
tion campaign.

Sales dipped again in the mid-1980s as the public woke up to
alcoholism, fetal alcohol syndrome, drunk driving, and the blessings
of personal fitness. After complaints about Thunderbird and Night
Train Express, Gallo promised to pull its high-alcohol wines from
stores in poor neighborhoods—but warned them first so they could
stock up. Sales rose again in 1991 as televised research lauded the
health benefits of red wine moderately consumed. In another year
revenues reached $849 million.

Gallo then bulldozed its way into Sonoma County, having
bought grapes from Napa for some time, and pleaded no contest in
1993, the year Julio died in a car accident, to a charge of passing off
cheap zinfandel from the Central Valley as a product of premium

fruit. In 1998, Sonoma grape pickers accused Gallo of substandard wages (only a ten-cent hourly increase in five years), poor working conditions, and union-busting.

Continuing its image games, Gallo used the Rutherford Vineyards brand name even though grapes for that wine came from Lodi. The wine was sold under an unauthorized photograph taken without permission on the idyllic property of Joseph Phelps, who threatened a lawsuit. Gallo also sold under brand names Louis M. Martini, Mirassou, Rancho Zabaco, Turning Leaf, Gossamer Bay, Indigo Hills, Burlwood, Copperidge, Liberty Creek, Peter Vella, Frei Brothers, MacMurray Ranch, Bridlewood Estate, Barefoot Cellars, William Hill, Canyon Road, and Charles Shaw. By this time other winemakers mimicked Gallo tactics: Korbel, for example, which marketed its sparkling wine as champagne.

Jennifer King of Plano, Texas sold "gallo" hand-painted ceramics with rooster patterns online to support herself and her diabetic daughter—until 2001, that is, when, to her incredulity and horror, Gallo's team of attorneys threatened to sue her.

Today Gallo's headquarters occupies a neoclassical "Parthenon West" or "temple on the Tuolumne," as locals variously describe it, behind a high wall lining Yosemite Boulevard. No visitors enter the gray, unlabeled structure watched by security guards and surveillance cameras, yet its very blankness shouts its unspoken influence over the entrenched castes of social life and city politics. The wine shipped from here was pressed from 48% of California's grape harvest. One of every four bottles of wine sold in the U.S. emerges here from behind concrete tinged green because mixed with ground glass from Thunderbird bottles. The word is that pay is low for everyone but top management and the hundred or so PhDs from U.C. Davis and Berkeley who work in the chemical lab.

When Joe Junior decided not to take his case to the U.S. Supreme Court, his biblically named grandson Micah said, "They took away our name, but we still know who we are." I wondered this about the people in decaying neighborhoods squatting in the literal and economic shadow of the Gallo building. A young black man drank what was obviously wine from a brown paper bag while leaning against his car in the driveway. Gallo statistics recently learned rolled behind my eyes: *seventy-five million cases of wine sold in 2005 alone at $3 billion in revenue.*

> Living in the Central Valley of California feels like stepping back into feudalism. The scattered towns stand in the valley like walled cities....The farmers are the peasants, working in the surrounding lands, shipping food off to urban centers. We live docile lives in the shadows of the nearby castles.
>
> – David "Mas" Masumoto

Ernest Gallo died in 2007. Since then the empire he left has embraced a number of eco-friendly practices and calls to conserve and recycle. Its best wines win contests here and abroad. Is it possible for a business with such a dreadful legacy and such a long record of deceptive and ruthless tactics to reform itself from within? Perhaps so. Some families do. Yet Gallo and other high-production wineries still reverse the ancient art by using enzymes and yeasts and marketing studies to produce what they think will sell—standardized, sweet, and smartly packaged—instead of selling what grows well locally.

Smaller specialty winemakers are relearning that a sensitive, patient focus on organics, biodynamics, single-vineyard bottling, and *terroir*, the French term for a discernible flavor bestowed by the unique characteristics of where a grape grows and ripens, pays off, financially and otherwise. It may well be that the future resides with *terroir* and not with an outdated factory model running low on cultural and ecological relevancy.

DO PLACES EVOLVE AND gain complexity from the people they attract? Is the real purpose of cities, villages, and settlements to do exactly this?

I had no answer, but as Kathy and I ascended the steps to the McHenry Museum, my eye caught a dark-haired docent in period dress: a shirtwaist in dark blue and cream, full skirts bearing a wheel-shaped floral imprint. Her smile drifted with her down the stairs... I had never really noticed how attractive these late-1800s outfits could be. Not wanting to stare, I forced my eyes to leave that pretty smile, moving upwards through a strange lethargy that slowed my steps.

The Museum, once a home, is now a repository of Modesto's historical documents. I sampled it, running my eyes over replica windmills, leafing through books, buying one, speaking with the docents, and taking notes. The dreamlike mood persisted.

Kathy seemed distracted when I reappeared at her side. She had been deep in discussion with a pony-tailed man wearing a ranger's badge. "Come back and visit us," he said with a certain emphasis as he moved off. Her face wore a look I had never seen there before.

"That docent seemed to like you," I noted, smiling.

She nodded as though distracted. "That was... really strong. Like being *drawn*..."

"Places will do that to you," I replied, remembering El Camino Real. "Modesto is getting at both of us. Can you feel it?"

She nodded as we descended the steps. The fair, dark-haired lady smiled at me again with a steady glance that went straight into me. Visions of farming and family drifted like potent tendrils of perfume through my imagination as we passed her and walked to the car. The power of the lure was impressive. Call it the What If, a geopsychic beckoning geared to penetrate any armor. *Why keep going when you could settle here?* a voice seemed to whisper seductively from the ground through my feet into my skull. *Isn't that what you've wanted: your own place, your own land, a wife to tend it with? What if you stayed a while? What if she's available? What if she's the one for you...*

Both hungry, we drove to a restaurant to eat, to clear our minds, and to reflect.

Seeing Kathy's dreamy-troubled expression, "You can still go back to the museum and get his phone number, you know," I pointed out.

Pause. Then: "What will happen if I do?"

"A day will come when the place is done with you, the spell lifts, and you wonder what you were thinking."

She shook her head in wonder.

"I've gotten tangled in this enough times to know how it goes. But there's no rule against entanglements." The look on her face tightened my heart in empathy.

"But why does it happen like this? It's so..." Her eyes were glittering.

I bit into a burger. "This is an example of what we've been calling 'ecotransference,' the power of a place to get to you. It wants your attention. It will reach right into your complexes and fascinations to get it. It induces the same sort of longing *it* possesses: to be noticed, to be appreciated, to be loved deeply..."

"How often has this happened to you?"

"Many times. It happened today. The woman in the skirt outside the museum."

She looked a question.

"I'm used to it, to the extent one can be."

"But it feels so crazy..."

"Yes. It can be overwhelming. This is why it's best not to work alone."

As we pulled out of the parking lot and headed for the freeway, I took a long look back toward the museum, wondering in spite of all past encounters what might have happened *this* time. I shook my head. What if.

GALLO WAS NOT THE only Modesto institution to rely on mass production.

To ordinary eyes, Kirby J. Hensley (1911-1999) had been an illiterate runaway from the backcountry of North Carolina. Still worse, he had lived and worked in Bakersfield. Yet to a growing number of believers, he was not only the Rebel from Modesto, but the one and only Modesto Messiah. Nobody held it against him that his wife worked for Campbell's Soup to pay the bills, or that he started his church in a garage: had not Jesus been born in a manger?

Hensley himself believed that God is whatever you think He is;

furthermore, "You are God!" In reverence of this truth, Hensley held mass ordinations of up to three thousand worshippers a day. Applicants were awarded prestigious titles: bishop, archbishop, deacon, deaconess, archpriest, cardinal, elder, right reverend, right sister, field missionary, monsignor, reverend mother, colonel, metropolitan, preceptor, abbot, abbess, evangelist, religious philosopher, apostolic scribe, and rabbi (applicants chose their own title). Those seeking and receiving ordination from his Universal Life Church included the Beatles, the Rolling Stones, S.I. Hayakawa, Rowan and Martin of *Laugh-In*, Goldie Hawn, Hugh Hefner, Mae West, Sammy Davis Jr., Milton Berle, Carol Burnett, Vicki Carr, Ray Bolger, Cyd Charisse, Doris Day, Jan Murray, Debbie Reynolds, Rosalind Russell, Barbara Streisand, Jimmy Stewart, and Mel Blanc, the voice of Donald Duck and Porky Pig. Hensley also ordained pets. His own title of Modesto Messiah was bestowed by amused psychology students at Sonoma State.

In retrospect it's difficult to know where the trouble began exactly. Perhaps with the $20,000 a day in contributions that came his way as his reputation spread. Perhaps with charges of operating a church illegally, issuing bogus honorary degrees, owing back taxes, and violating the California Education Code. Perhaps with the Universal Life Church's collection of a healthy percentage once a believer's monthly income topped $1,000. "Heaven," Hensley stated sonorously in perfect Americanese, "is when you have what you want, and Hell is when you don't have it."

Certainly no one could find fault with Hensley's fund of energy. In 1964 and 1968 he ran for President of the United States courtesy of his own Universal Party as chartered by his own constitution. The Party doctrine held that Earth was being helped by friendly extraterrestrials to achieve universal brotherhood. Party members claimed to have been contacted by UFOs and to be in touch with them telepathically. Hensley gave thanks: "We live in a great time, because Man now is breaking his bondage with Earth." His campaign promises included redeemable $15 tickets issued for doing things right instead of citations for doing things wrong. Positive psychologists could claim him as their pioneer.

Nonbelievers said that Hensley was a bad fit for frugal Valley values and culture, but I wonder. Like Coyote, Hensley was a marvelous parodist, evangelizing with a hammer whose exaggerated swings knocked old idols to pieces. Beyond that, the drive-through marriages he conducted unfolded rapidly on rooftops, in fields, and even on the backs of motorcycles. That last location strangely in sync with the *circulatio* motif rolling on in Modesto.

Stockton (*labyrinth*)

"Stockton is a labyrinth..." Kathy said. Trust someone who resonated with Ariadne to spot one in no time flat.

She pointed at an elaborate filigree decorating one side of an administrative building, then gestured down the street toward a maze of grills, ledges, window frames, cornices, and lattices interlocking with each other as they ran out of sight. A corporate logo on a nearby window folded three yellow angles into each other. I thought about the canal downtown, with its layers, fences, and locks, and about where it led: to one of the largest inverted deltas in the world. Inverted because it narrowed to a funnel instead of widening out. Stockton lay caught within its web.

"...that dead ends."

That too made sense. After tripling between 1998 and 2005, home prices here had plummeted as the housing boom deflated into a bust. The foreclosure rate was the highest in the nation. Across U.S. cities, Stockton ranked in the bottom seven worst for commute times, unemployment, income tax rates, and violent crime. Of seventeen cities, Stockton was the only one with more dropouts than graduates for 2006-07. Only 15% of adults here held a college degree.

Stockton was trying. Here downtown, the new San Joaquin County Administration Building presented a glittering six-level example of what original design could do: in this case consolidate sixteen different service and support departments previously scattered across the city. Incorporating historical landmarks, the building had been completed ahead of schedule and under its projected budget. Its irregular facade of translucent green glass echoed "transparency!" into the streets. Its steel framework was visible through the glass.

A glance around disclosed other innovative projects. Unlike so many other downtowns I had visited across California, the streets were clean here. They held a feeling that new things were being planned, new possibilities entertained. There might yet be a path out of the maze.

For this trip we had driven out of Contra Costa County along State Route 4, making our way eastward through Pittsburg and Antioch, the scars left by mining still visible on the flank of Mt. Diablo, through Oakley, with its graffiti, prefab tracts, trailer park, and Statues & Stuff, past undeveloped fields green and luminous after last week's rain. We had seen lots for sale, sidewalks alternating with dirt paths, then, out by Brentwood, higher-end neighborhoods behind thick stone-faced walls giving way to storage complexes, auto parts stores, a Designer Dogs, a church named Soul's Harbor, pest control signs, and acres of tracts where peaches, strawberries, blackberries, cherries, apricots, nectarines, and corn once flourished. A few miles beyond Terminous we turned south on I-5 for Stockton.

We made it in time for the spring Asparagus Festival. Crowds of people clustered in and around the Events Center, but we had no trouble finding parking on Weber. We saw police everywhere, even in boats on the lake.

Agriculture constitutes San Joaquin County's primary income. According to the 2007 Agriculture Commissioner's Crop Report, milk brought in $466.1 million, grapes $216.9 million, cherries $201.7 million, almonds $158.9 million, walnuts $129.4 million, tomatoes $125.4 million, and cattle $103.5 million. Other major crops included hay, nursery and woody ornamentals, apples, and asparagus. No county in the United States produced more asparagus or walnuts. San Joaquin was also the leading producer of cherries, apples, corn, and pumpkins. All told, revenue from agriculture came to $6.6 billion.

Stockton, formerly French Camp, Weberville, Embarcadero, Tuleberg, Tent City, Brick City, and Town of Cloth Shanties, is the county seat. In 1843, William Gulnac applied for a land grant here and traded it, all forty-nine thousand acres, to his merchandising partner Charles Weber in exchange for a $60 grocery bill (some said a bar bill, Gulnac having been a notorious drunk). After several name changes the town got its latest from the American commodore and Know Nothing Party member Robert F. Stockton, who briefly played Theseus by rescuing Weber, now a rancher, from a Californio jail in Los Angeles. In 1847 Weber bought the sloop *Maria* to ferry supplies upriver.

A risky undertaking. Many ships wrecked in the crooked channels of the delta, including the *Sagamore*, the *American Eagle*, and the *Stockton*. By 1852, the Sacramento and San Joaquin rivers that meet here flowed sluggishly from silt and debris washed into them from hydraulic mining for gold in the Sierras. The watery route linking Stockton to the sea fifty miles away ran brown and muddy. Its shallowness raised recurring floods that overtopped levees. Only after many delays could engineers finally deepen the channel.

Levees had been raised since the 1860s, but in time they too proved problematic. If engineers dug the building material from inside the levee line, they could expect subsidence. Dredging for fill from the outside destabilized the levees as well as any buildings placed on them. By the twentieth century not only these maze walls but entire islands would sink into geological depression.

Here David Young assembled the centennial harvester in 1876, making Stockton a center of mechanized farming. Here was where the Fresno scraper was experimented with before a modified version dug the Panama Canal, and where blacksmith James Porteous, who made the modifications, patented forty-six other inventions. The Holt Brothers set up the Stockton Wheel Company to make carriages, a link-belt combine, a sidehill combine with an adjustable mower, and, in 1904, the caterpillar tread for moving heavy loads over peat. The British took the idea and began machining together secret armored vehicles code-named "cisterns," "reservoirs," and eventually "tanks" for use in the deserts of Egypt.

The clamshell dredge, the Atlas plow, and the Hume reel were also invented here in territory favored by the spirit of Daedalus, the skilled god who built the minotaur-containing labyrinth. The Norse knew him as the smith god Volund, the Anglo-Saxons as Weyland.

> The Delta of Central California is a study in V-shapes. Wedges of winging waterfowl seem to match the lines of wave wash ever-widening from ship stem to shore. Vessels' bows and tackle point skyward in clusters of giant triangles, and the very boundary lines of the Delta form a nearly-equilateral triangular mass.
>
> – Nicholas Hardeman

On the side of a building a mural depicted Native Californian craftsmen sawing trees, chiseling a stone, and building a wall.

Outside the Asparagus Festival we were handed free brochures telling us how to obtain documents for

* DIVORCE * LIVING TRUST * INCORPORATIONS

* EVICTION SERVICES * MOBILE NOTARY

This legal documents service was provided by Andrew's, the same name as a church we had visited earlier. In another, St. John's, we were inadvertently locked inside after the service ended. We had come to inspect a stained glass depiction of an angel pointing beyond John the Evangelist at the shining gates of the New Jerusalem. "They look like a dam," Kathy said. *Or the locks of a canal*, I thought just before hearing the church doors being bolted shut by the pastor.

The Port of Stockton linking the Central Valley to the Pacific Ocean smelled like oil and resembled a factory built and staffed by giants. After the Valley's first cargo boat waddled up and down the San Joaquin River in 1846, Joan Doak set up a ferry station here two years later. In another year the *John A. Sutter* became the first paddle wheeler to reach Stockton, soon to grow into a supply depot for the Gold Rush, but the riverboat days were drawing to a close, especially after construction of the San Joaquin and Kings River canals in 19871 and the arrival of the Central Pacific soon after. (Having done so much dam-building, hydroelectricity pioneer John Eastwood would die in the Kings River in 1924 while trying to save a woman from drowning.)

The Port came into its own in the depths of the Great Depression, but it had to await more dredging before the largest vessels could arrive there. Deep-ocean ships sailing across the flat land of the Valley must have startled many a farmer. Today the Port occupies eight hundred and nine hectares and berths seventeen large vessels. Seven-point-seven million square feet of warehousing for dry and wet bulk goods connect to I-5 and several other freeways (Stockton is a transit hub), the Union Pacific, and the Burlington Northern Santa Fe. The dredged channel descends to thirty-seven feet at low tide. An ad suggested, "A pregnant note to shippers: Profit by our berth controls!" Goods were funneled here from many locations like water through converging Delta channels.

I was disappointed to be denied entrance by the security guard. The Port, she informed me politely, was off limits to unauthorized civilians, even if they were writers. Over a maze of high fences crowned with barbed wire I glimpsed grain silos, gargantuan pipes, oversized drums of cable, steam, wire, cylindrical train cars, leaning power poles... It felt like one big machine. Or a game board with mechanical pieces. I remembered the warehouse-sized Toys "R" Us we had passed after driving under a tangle of freeway overpasses. The storefront had been guarded by life-sized wooden soldiers.

Stockton. Storage warehouses, cargo containers, enclosed tanks, military depots, grain elevators, freight cars. It all reminded me of the city-sized sealed storage cities of Arthur Clark's fictional Rama spaceship. A Latino graduate student of mine who had grown up here summed it up in a word: "Isolated." "Nothing to show us," he added, "that there's a world out there beyond." A steel bubble that transcended ethnicity; everyone and everything in boxes. "Nobody wants to start a life there." A pervasive mood of hopelessness. And yet those immense, toylike shapes on the horizon once over the river bridge on SR-4. Toy stores, a children's museum, a ball park and arena, and tractors, scaffolds, and girders stacked as though by some busy god's Erector Set. The streets were named after generals and presidents, but gang members drove and roamed them now in a futile quest to grow up. On I-5 one billboard shouted "PLAY" (in a casino) and the next, "Don't Serve Alcohol to Teens."

ALCHEMISTS LIKE NICOLAS FLAMMEL often compared engaging in the Great Work with negotiating an intricate maze. Sometimes they called the opus Solomon's Labyrinth after the great temple-builder of antiquity. On woodcuts a chemical apparatus occupied the center of the design and was ringed about with walls like levees. In some versions towers stood in the background.

The labyrinth image hinted at important questions. How to stay enclosed long enough in the laboratory to finish the Great Work of transformation and power? How to get out once again?

Alchemists also worked with the archetypal image of the Net. Chemically this meant concocting a crystalline alloy of antimony and copper. For the more reflective alchemists who used their art as a wisdom tradition, laboratory, maze, and net were not separate from alchemist, apparatus, flame, and water, but part of one meaningful weave.

The Sacramento-San Joaquin River Delta spreads netlike through nearly six hundred thousand acres of peat, silt, tules, and mud. Before its thousand-plus miles of canals were installed, Miwok, Wintun, Yokuts, and Maidu fished here for generations. The Maidu helped Reuben Kercheval build the first levee on Grand Island in 1849. Hudson Bay Company trappers sought beaver here. The peat, a rich, loamy legacy of perennial growth and decomposed water plants, grew asparagus, celery, corn, tomatoes, potatoes, Bartlett pears, corn, and many other crops like magic.

Once surrounded by riparian forests, wetlands, and prairie, the Delta estuary's function as a filter has vastly degraded. Between them the State Water Project and the Central Valley Project draw down from the Delta five million gallons of freshwater *per minute*. Forty percent of California's drinking water and 45% of its agricultural irrigation depend on this shrinking estuary now poisoned by runoff and threatened by saltwater incursions from San Francisco Bay. As the Delta backs up, no longer able to handle a full third of California's total drainage, dried-out soil blows away in destructive "peat storms." Accumulations of salts and heavy metals threaten Delta smelt, longfin smelt, salmon, striped bass, threadfin shad, and humans who drink the water. Thousands of fish that survive this chemical brew end up shredded in pumps.

This decline came to public attention during the drought years of 1987-1992, when water quality deteriorated and the Delta smelt and chinook salmon were on the verge dying off. Environmentalists fought for them, agribusinesses demanded water, the State Water Resources Control Board found itself caught between them, and Congress enacted the Central Valley Project Improvement Act to reallocate some water to protect fragile ecosystems.

In 1994, a group of state and federal agencies—twenty-five by 2000—formed CALFED to decide what to do about the Delta. Measurements were taken and scientists consulted. A Bay-Delta Accord began working on increasing the reliability of Delta water. A new California Bay-Delta Authority oversaw CALFED. After complaints that CALFED exercised insufficient leadership, Governor Schwarzenegger, who favored a southward-running "peripheral canal" that avoided the Delta, initiated an independent review. From this came a ten-year action plan and various recommendations.

In December 2008, a suit was brought in Sacramento Superior Court seeking to stop water from being drawn from the Delta until its ecosystems were stable, and to stop irrigation of soils naturally high in selenium like those in the Westlands in Merced County.

A week later, the Westlands Water District joined with other districts to file a suit to block water reductions imposed by the California Department of Fish and Game. As these battles played out, populations of Delta smelt and threadfin shad dropped to record lows. In a year the Sacramento and San Joaquin Rivers were labeled endangered. By 2010 water allotments for agriculture were increased once again.

Billionaires Stewart and Lynda Resnick, owners of Roll International, had owned cropland in the Valley since buying it from Texaco and Mobile in the 1980s. To irrigate this land and its pistachio and almond trees, the Resnicks contracted for water deliveries from the Delta via the California Aqueduct. Through their Westside Mutual Water Company they also bought twenty thousand acres of state property that was supposed to serve as an underground Kern Water Bank charged with one million acre-feet. They also controlled key water districts. Their company Paramount Agribusiness grew more almonds and pistachios than any competitor in the world.

To support their efforts to privatize water in California, the Resnicks persuaded Senator Dianne Feinstein to hand President Obama a letter from them instructing him to loosen environmental regulations and allocate more water to growers. Until this flagrant event few had heard of the Resnicks, but their other holdings were better known: Fiji Water, Suterra, Paramount, Teleflora, the Neptune Pacific Line, and Pom Wonderful, recently investigated by the Food and Drug Administration for making false health claims. The Center for Biological Diversity and six other plaintiffs have filed a lawsuit against the Resnicks for selling public water for a profit. Kern County has also filed a suit to find out why the water table near the underground bank has dropped a hundred and fifteen feet in just three years.

Growers often frame protection from further damage to the Delta as a "fish versus farmers" dispute. What matters more, economic growth or the life of a smelt? The smelt's possible extinction does not constitute a solitary event, however. At issue is the decline of precious, irreplaceable biodiversity as species perish on every continent. To demand sane limits on how much water is exported from the Delta for agriculture does not threaten growers with failure. In fact, as the water table fell and homes went belly up all over the San Joaquin Valley, the Resnicks grew their revenues.

As for the Delta, the shredding of its nets and webs of life does not go without rising human cost.

> Standing by the Glacier vending machine in Lost Hills one day, I met a 19-year-old woman from Michoacán who migrated to Chicago at age nine with her family before relocating to Lost Hills in 2008. She works a night shift, from 5 p.m. to 3 a.m., picking bell peppers for $8 an hour. If she works hard, she said, in a month she can save $300. Asked if she drinks the tap water in her home she said no, that "it tastes nasty and they tell us not to drink it." So every three days she fills up her jug. On a blazing July day, she pushed her full, 5-gallon jug of drinking water from the vending machine back to her house in a baby carriage. About two hundred yards down the road, the California Aqueduct was full and flowing fast.
>
> – John Gibler

Ultimately, industrialized agriculture remains fundamentally unsustainable. It destroys plants, animals, soils, and communities. It converts natural resources into overpopulation, as the Green Revolution so clearly demonstrated. Control, accumulation, and domination as ends in themselves represent a pathological state of possession by machinelike thought. Agriculture, a means to these ends, conducts an anti-alchemy that reduces the living to the dead, throws natural cycles into chaos, devolves the healing to the putrified.

The fall of civilizations reveals a strangely consistent attitude behind their demise: a narcissistic unwillingness to see oneself as dependent on the natural nets supporting every step and every breath. Sumer fell when irrigation brought salt to the surface of once-fertile soils. Rome fell after miners digging silver struck a water table that flooded. No more money to pay the military contractors propping up the Western Empire. The cult of the self-made man takes hold just before his hubris finishes him off, for in the natural world he represents an unfortunate and unsuccessful evolutionary anomaly.

When the water stops and the soil dies of thirst, when the croplands sink and the levees tremble into dust, not even Daedalus can save reckless Icarus from descent.

ON A LATER TRIP to Stockton I passed through a long strip mall named Tracy, which means "warlike." On North Central and West Tenth stood rows of brick buildings: sure indications of a town that's burned a lot. "Lake of Fire" announced a sign above an Italian restaurant as monuments here and there praised firefighters of the past. In mythology tricksters bring fire, but here a dead coyote (a common trickster figure) lay along Route 205 just outside the city. Above the old downtown around Sixth rose a compensatory water tower.

In Stockton I stayed near French Camp, a former nook for trappers. Across town, choking and sneezing residents were trying to stop Olivera Egg Ranch from adding more sludge to a sixteen-acre lake of chicken manure. After years of complaints, the Humane Society was now involved as well. I parked in a relatively new but already desolate neighborhood some developer had poured from a mold and left to harden. The very pavement exuded loneliness.

The hotel offered me a choice of Starbucks, Seven Eleven, and four fast food joints; I chose none of the above and went for a walk instead. As dusk fell, warehouses receded to the horizon. Trucks roared by, temporarily outshouting rock music blaring unexpectedly from within a loading dock. Weed-covered fields pointed nowhere. Everything felt empty and on hold, although a tour of the low-water native-planting demonstration garden maintained by the Master Gardeners of Stockton cheered me a little. If only Stockton could learn to trust its own history: that of creative invention.

I could come to no conclusion about Stockton, where *condensatio*, *coagulatio*, and *distillatio* had assumed, at least for now, all the corners, lines, and angles of an labyrinthine, automated factory gone mad. Surely some local Ariadne stood by to help with threading the maze on both land and water, solving the riddle, lifting this place out of its vacuum-packed box of depression. I did not know whether to hope for that before or after the walls fell down.

Part Two:
Sacramento Valley
(Yellowing and Reddening)

Sacramento (*mortificatio*)

> To the conventional wisdom that one ought never
> to build on a floodplain, California has responded
> with its capital city.
>
> – John McPhee

Within the Great Central Valley of California simmer a broad range
of alchemical reductions and, mixed in with them, mythologems
sparkling and dark. A mere 4% of the Valley's original landscape has
yet to be transformed. Seven million acres have changed into urban
and suburban hardtop just since 1964. Containment levees against
uncontrolled *solutio* stand in Bakersfield, the Delta, Stockton, and
Sacramento because streets in these places sit below stream beds.
Hardpan seals the Central Valley retort from below; lines of mountains form its outer walls. As with any enclosed alchemical vessel,
getting in is easier than getting out.

Between sphincter and maze, or Fort Tejon and Stockton,
stretches two hundred and sixty-eight miles of San Joaquin Valley.
Another fifty miles brought us to Sacramento.

As the upper chamber of the world's longest retort, the
Sacramento Valley's seven thousand square miles hold three million

137

occupants, dozens of major crops, various heavy industries, one international airport, and one deep-water port. This valley receives twice as much precipitation as its counterpart to the south, keeps a little cooler on average despite its hot summers, and, though flat, undulates here and there. The Sutter Buttes, remains of an extinct volcano, rise in a circle forty-four miles north of the state capital. For two years of the 1960s, Titan ICBMs stood at the base of the Buttes. The ancient Maidu believed that the souls of the dead gathered at the peaks. These modest heights of a few thousand feet oversaw a universal sea until the land appeared and people began to arrive thanks to the labors of Earthmaker and Coyote.

Gabriel Moraga arrived in October of 1808. Considering the flood-prone valley with its long, Delta-bound river, its clustered native villages stained red by drying salmon, Moraga finished Communion and picked a place name in remembrance of the Eucharist, a Sacrament ending in sacrifice.

"Captain" John Sutter washed into the Sacramento Valley in 1839, which was six years after a malaria epidemic carried in by trappers killed thousands of Miwoks. He was running from a legacy of debt reaching all the way back to his abandoned wife and children in Switzerland. The "Captain" title was for appearances. He had never been an officer, but his extensive traveling and hustling had taught him the value of a reputation.

Departing the *Clementine* in the company of ten Hawaiians and a slave boy sold to him by Kit Carson, Sutter came determined to establish his own little country with himself as emperor. Passports, currency, royal colors, the works. To that end he used his eloquence—for he had the devil's own tongue and the extraversion to go with it—to get himself invited in 1839 to U.S. Consul and spy Thomas O. Larkin's Fourth of July party, where Sutter met Mexican-appointed Governor Juan Bautista de Alvarado. Given Alvarado's reputation as a chronic drinker, he was likely well lubricated by the time Sutter battened onto him and asked the Governor of California for a land grant.

After the party he also found money to construct a fort (equipped with a dungeon for enemies of the empire) in the place he named New Helvetia on a bank of the American River. To the Nisenan Maidu and Miwok he introduced himself as Columbus and Cortés before him had to native ambassadors they encountered: with the carrot of shiny gifts and the stick of cannon fire to intimidate them. He then proceeded to use gossip and innuendo to turn them against each other long enough to siphon off laborers to build his fort. When protests arose, he countered by threatening to attack any villages to which his busy new serfs returned. He fed them bran sifted from wheat and the offal of slaughtered animals.

For a time life seemed to flow tranquilly at New Helvetia, at least from Sutter's privileged vantage. Once his blacksmith had forged a tin coin with star for use as Indian currency, he was able to pay them with it and demand that they buy goods at his store. He grew wheat, barley, corn; trapped beaver, caught salmon, hunted deer, raised cattle; ran a tailor shop, tannery, stable, and smithy; and sold passports and plots of land to non-naturalized Americans in direct violation of Californio immigration law. When the Hudson Bay Company arrived, he built a distillery to trade liquor for their furs at a profit. His hired men walked about in uniforms obtained from the Russians departing Fort Ross on the coast. They had come to trap otters. He bought their fort on credit.

A problem cropped up in 1844 when Sutter founded Sutterville on the Sacramento River three miles downstream from the American River. Recognizing his attempt as yet another encroachment, the Miwoks fought back. Sutter responded by capturing Raphero, their leader, and posting his head on a pike outside the gate of the fort. The Miwok warriors fell back but continued to raid and skirmish, forcing Sutter to spend resources to guard his property and men.

He could no longer afford this, having incurred much debt once again through extravagant living and colonial operations like the Fort Ross purchase, so he made a treaty with the Kolomas to allow him to build a new sawmill. He also made peace with the Yalesumni, who helped Sutter employee John Marshall of New Jersey dig a deeper tailrace for the mill. The builders had sunk the wheel too low. Sutter needed the mill to get out of debt by selling

lumber to American settlers who had heard of New Helvetia's lavish hospitality. Their numbers increased from trickle to flood once
word spread of Marshall's 1848 discovery of gold in the tailrace.

The Miwok strategy of gradually bleeding Sutter financially
now paid off. Overwhelming crowds of gold hunters turned his fort
into a gambling hall and bazaar and his land into fields of pock-
marks and craters. Squatters sat down where they pleased and took
what they wanted, even down to the millstones. Sutter could control none of it, and therefore could profit from none of it, let alone
pay his lengthening bar bill. The Californio government refused to
help enforce his rights because of how he had subverted the law of
the land. The Russians wanted their money. The cacophony reached
an unbearable height when Sutter's abandoned family unexpectedly arrived looking for him. Signing over all his remaining property to
his newly discovered son, John Sutter Senior fled to Coloma.

Before he left, he tasked his son with founding another city, this
time at the confluence of two icy rivers.

WITHOUT OUR HAVING PLANNED it, our arrival in Sacramento coin-
cided with the hundred-and-fortieth anniversary of when the
Union and Continental Pacific Railroads met here to complete a
transcontinental connection. One word had been spoken to celebrate the last spike penetrating the ground: "Done." In Old
Sacramento, docents in black top hats and coattails reenacted the
event near the California State Railroad Museum.

We drove here on I-80, coming eastward past "El Dorado" casino ads on billboards until the gray, toothy skyline rose up in the distance beyond flat fields still green with crops. A few minutes north
on I-5 brought us into Old Sacramento, a historical park on the east
bank of the Sacramento River. Cars parked in front of the Old
West-style structures. So much had ended here: transcontinental
rail, wagon train, stage coach, river boat, telegraph, California Trail,
and Pony Express, which found its western terminus at a bank in
town.

Breweries and saloons had once dominated this neighborhood, but the golden cup had passed to tourist shops and boutiques. Everyone seemed to want money for something: shops, peddlers on and off the street, even machines, but I couldn't get any cash at the Historic Museum or the Wells Fargo up the road.

On display in the railroad museum we found hardware once sold by merchants but now clamped behind glass cases. We saw hammers, saws, shovels, tongs, vices, pliers, hooks, hinges, barrels for beer, and bigger engines of industry like the river dredge on display mouth-downward outside.

The city's first official map displayed a square fitted into the lower-right angle formed by the north-south Sacramento River and the east-west American. In the center of the square squatted the State Capitol. Around it German and Swiss immigrants ran breweries while manufacturers sold supplies to outgoing Gold Rush miners and weighed and bought what gold could be taken out of cold riverbanks. Ships docked along the waterfront served as retailers, hotels, and manufacturers; one, the *Whiton*, became the city post office, and another, the *La Grange*, was stripped down and converted into a prison.

SAMUEL BRANNAN OF MAINE had been on the move since age nineteen, a would-be land speculator and town builder gone bust. He became a Mormon to realize "far more prophet" (his words) than he'd been able to scrounge thus far. By 1844 he had married the daughter of a wealthy Mormon widow and, a few months later, the sister of a church leader.

Even before the Gold Rush President Polk and his congressional allies had their eagle eyes fixed on the acquisition of California and Texas. Brannan managed to involve himself in a secret plan backed by businessmen and various politicians, possibly including Polk, for the Mormons to settle in California, where they could advance American interests. To that end Elder Brannan led his flock aboard a sailing ship and departed from New York. On the way he would guide hopeful settlers into a covenant requiring three years of labor from them as a return on his investment.

When the colonists reached San Francisco they found other Americans already in possession of the city, so they detoured into the San Joaquin Valley and began hammering together a colony named New Hope on the north bank of the Stanislaus. By then, though, Brigham Young had killed the plan in favor of colonizing Utah. Most of the Mormons abandoned New Hope, covenant or no covenant; some found work helping build Sutter's new sawmill.

Brannan heard about the gold strike at Sutter's Mill from his dry goods business partner C.C. Smith. The two quickly bought up all the picks, blankets, and shovels available and sold them out of Sutter's Fort at hugely elevated prices. From the fort led a road to an embarcadero just south of the mouth of the American River. Ships had anchored there to offload cargo where logging cottonwoods for the fort had left a clearing in 1840. Brannan and another partner, P. B. Cornwall, put up tents of goods in this spot to sell goods to miners on their way up the river. Around this clearing would collect Old Sacramento. Sutter still owned it, but he owed Brannan money. Incoming ships secured themselves to waterfront tree limbs.

Before Sutter fled to Coloma he had convinced John Junior and merchant Samuel Hensley to hire an engineer to survey and plat "Sacramento City" next to the fort at the junction of the American and the Sacramento Rivers. They offered attorney Peter Burnett a quarter of gross proceeds from land sales in exchange for being their land agent. Unfortunately for them, ferry operator George McDougal sat on a lease for the entire waterfront—a docked ship of his had been the first semi-permanent structure in town; and, positioned a few miles to the south, Sutterville posed a competitive threat as well, especially when McDougal moved there in retaliation for a legal action initiated to dislodge him of the waterfront.

As a first step, Brannan and his merchant allies arranged for McDougal's stock to be destroyed to put him out of business. Second, they convinced Sutterville's land agent, Lansford Hastings, that they too planned to exit Sacramento City. When Hastings offered them eighty free lots, Brannan talked John Sutter Jr. into topping this offer to keep them from moving. John Junior gave them

80% of all town lots, which came to five hundred choice spots to expand their businesses. This stratagem terminated Sutterville (except for its brewery, which closed later) and handed Sacramento City over to the merchants and entrepreneurs. By the end of 1849, lot prices had jumped from $250 to $8,000. Brannan and John S. Fowler bought a flour mill built by Sutter and made it over into the Hotel de France. On its opening day they poured free wine and whiskey and threw baskets of champagne from the balcony.

> Only months before, it had been a flour mill. Bought and moved to the new city by Samuel Brannan and John Fowler, the city's new transportation mogul, the two men simply changed the old mill from pro-cessing flour to processing would-be miners. To Brannan and Fowler, the thousands of hopeful young men passing through Sacramento on their way to the gold fields were human grist for their economic mill.
>
> – Mark Eiffler

Where Native Californians had traded dentalium shells as cur-rency and gambled for fun, Sacramento founded itself and then expanded itself on the principle of business at any human or eco-logical cost. Hugely inflated prices for goods doubled, and redou-bled, and again without limit; coins paid out for gold went at a 50% markup. Passengers sailing from San Francisco were charged from 200% to 3,000% of what voyages of that length normally cost. Like later state governors such as Arnold Schwarzenegger, the high rollers lived in hotels. Dr. John Morse wrote from Sacramento:

> ...Everything in and about the city indicated an overwhelming business, conducted without a par-ticle of method and in such utter confusion and recklessness of manner as to make it impossible for a man to construct calculations that embraced more than the contingencies of a single day.

Why such utter chaos? California became a U.S. territory in 1848. The provisional state constitution of 1849 enabled a speculator's paradise by leaving commerce unregulated and its laws unenforced. As a result, gambling did not confine itself to halls set aside for Monte, Faro, or poker. Just about everyone speculated, from merchants to bankers to lawyers to barkeeps, cops, missionaries, hookers, miners, realtors, and the retailers who sold the miners tools for ten times their worth. The near-total lack of ethical conduct in the majority of transactions quickly became the norm, with honesty always suspect; speculators and their victims alike would have spurned the charming notion—still prevalent today—that business allowed to ravage without scruple will somehow regulate itself.

Accounts from that time document "confusion," "dimness," "darkness," and "plunder" covering every available surface with bottles, boxes, barrels, lumber, machinery. Food lay spoiling as people played cards. Gaming was ubiquitous, and manic, found in bars, hotels, on docks, and on street corners. Not just Monte and Faro, but euchre, ninepins, whist, bear-and-bull fights (hence the Wall Street terminology), and what would now be known as Russian Roulette. Miners called what they did in the gold fields "the Great California Lottery."

> Two ex-ministers of the gospel were conspicuous among the gamesters, one dealing monte, and the other playing at faro. The game of poker was indulged in on a magnificent scale by the heavier capitalists, three thousand dollars being lost or won without creating unusual excitement. Such was the ascendancy of gambling then that the leaders of the craft were men of great influence, and, for a while, almost controlled the policy of the city.
>
> – Paula Bowden

As residents crammed into boardinghouses and hotels, landowners and speculators extracted money for squatting, espe-

cially from homeless "overlanders" newly arrived by covered wagon.
Police who could not be bothered to enforce the laws accepted bank
money for carrying out forced evictions.

> The first criminal conviction we find noted is that
> of John Row, November 8, 1849, who was convict-
> ed of stealing a heifer, worth about twenty dollars,
> and sentenced to pay therefor a fine of two hundred
> dollars, and costs amounting to three hundred and
> fifteen dollars, making at total of five hundred and
> fifteen dollars.
>
> —Paula Bowden

When enough residents grew outraged at the disorganized
tumult, they protested the high prices charged for city lots by forming a Settlers' Association and publishing a list of twenty-five of the
worst looters and land sharks nominated "Men of Remarkable
Principles." The merchants, speculators, and bankers thus targeted
responded by appointing themselves to the first city council and
starting up a "Law and Order Party" to dominate city politics by
stuffing ballot boxes. So firmly did the city's new ruling elite
depress wages, and so stubbornly did they deprive services for
health and sanitation of necessary funding, that by the winter of
1850, three quarters of Sacramento's population lay sick in their
beds from illnesses like dysentery, scurvy, and cholera brought in on
the plush riverboat *New World*. The dead went unburied because
their families could not afford the coffins stacked up like empty barrels awaiting cargo. Goods lay moldering in shops and warehouses
as laborers died or went broke.

Overlander members of the Settlers' Association had gotten
practice writing bylaws, rotating leadership, and circulating public
notices out on the long trails to California. This practice stood them
in good stead now. One overlander, Dr. Charles Robinson, who rec-
ommended complying with all just laws but no unjust ones, found
himself nominated an Association spokesman. When the courts
continued their passivity and the new city council proved as cor-

rupt as the old, Association membership picked up, and picked up arms.

To an angry party gathered to protect the Madden property from foreclosure Mayor Bigelow issued false assurances of cooperation that blew their anger into fury once Association leaders were taken into custody. One hothead, John "Shoot the Mayor!" Maloney, started the Squatter Riots that left four dead (including Maloney) and five wounded. Robinson was imprisoned on the brig for a time, and the mayor left for San Francisco and died there of cholera. Squatters were now demonized as criminals by the Law and Order Party, and the Association fell apart.

So, however, did the house of cards stacked by financial elites whose bills were coming due as their eastern suppliers called them in. The elites' calculated wealth, it turned out, rested on the gigantic gamble of inflated figures. Land values inflated by 1,000% plummeted, small businessmen went out of business, the bankers went next, and the merchants after them. When the city's largest landholder declared bankruptcy, much of the corrupt power structure subsided with it just in time for the floods of the early 1850s.

Sutter's holdings were gone; he would succumb to a lonely, debt-ridden, alcoholic death, as would James Marshall and Samuel Brannan. (By contrast, Robinson became the first governor of Kansas after fighting off pro-slavery opposition. He remained active and productive far into old age.) The city council had been swept away by its own colossal malfeasance. The gambling run that called itself the city's economy had ended, overspent.

In November of 1852, the year of another flood, a fire burned down almost all of the city. But by 1854 and the breaking of the Gold Rush fever, Sacramento was sheathing itself in brick, crops were growing round about, people had actual homes to live in, and merchants were exchanging hard currency at prices close to fair.

SEVERED AT THE WRISTS, two immense white hands hovering over a fountain shook to close an unspecified deal.

Banks surrounded us, as Kathy pointed out: Comerica Bank,

recipient of two billion dollars in TARP federal bailout money and picketed by fired Detroit workers demanding severance pay. American River Bank, posted on the bankruptcy watch list. Wells Fargo, buyer of its competitor Watchovia after receiving a bailout. U.S. Bank, seizer of homes (like Wells Fargo and Bank of America) but blocked in the highest court in Massachusetts. Bank of the West, target of numerous consumer complaints for charging unexpected fees at will. Wedbush, poised for takeovers of other companies but too cheap to issue credit cards to its employees. Bank of America, bailout recipient, doubler of credit card interest rates, aggressive forecloser, and target of Wikileaks accusations of massive, systemic corruption. Lawyers here too like remoras seen near sharks: Perkins & Associates, Seyfarth & Shaw, McDonough, Holland & Allen.

To the west, office buildings on either side of the Capitol Mall on which we stood in wonder rose up as one set of gates framing another: the two towers of the Art Deco bridge over the Sacramento River. The towers had been painted gold. To the east, the Mall led straight to the Capitol behind which were memorials so numerous I lost count. Late May heat deflected off white facades and glass panels drew sweat down our faces.

"I think," I remarked, "we may be in Hell."

"I keep recalling lyrics," replied Kathy after a moment, having cooled her feet in a fountain, "that followed me here. Chris Rea's 'The Road to Hell.'"

> Well I'm standing by a river
> But the water doesn't flow
> It boils with every poison you can think of....
>
> And the perverted fear of violence
> Chokes a smile on every face
> And common sense is ringing out the bells
> This ain't no technological breakdown
> Oh no, this is the road to Hell...

Unlike most indigenous mythologies, some originating in the West distinguish between the Afterlife (Hades, Sheol, Limbo) and a darker place where the monstrous and evil end up. For the Greeks, Tartarus, a river-fed pit below the great palace of Hades, held the fifty-headed giants, the Titan Cronus, who ate his children, the ravenously hungry Cyclopes, and the winged serpent Typhon, a beast so immense and powerful that he threatened the Olympians. Proud Sisyphus was there rolling his rock uphill and watching it roll down; Ixion the seducer, bound on a wheel of fire; and Tantalus the dismemberer, forever tormented by fruit just out of reach.

For the Norse, Hel ("hides, conceals") was both a realm and the name of its grim keeper. On the far side of a bridge, enormous gates guarded a hall of treasure and a cock whose crowing will announce the end of the world. The ancient Hebrews spoke of Gehenna, a barren valley filled with idolaters, their false gods, the burnt bodies of capital criminals, and Moloch, the bull god whom priests fed with children. The New Testament also speaks of Gehenna; Muslims call it Jahannam. Virgil's triple-walled Hell stood on adamantine pillars.

By the time of Augustine four centuries after the Lamb of God had been condemned by religious hypocrites and slaughtered, these grim realms, combined with Egyptian tales of a final judgment, crystalized into Christendom's literalized Hell.

Jung believed Hell to be archetypal. Perhaps. Here it certainly was unregulated. The waterfront whose store-ships were visited by floats made out of old hulls sculling about like Charon's ferries was intended by citizens to remain a commons, but by 1854, the California Steam Navigation Company monopolized it, only to be bought in turn by the Central Pacific in 1873. The railroad plotted by Huntington, Hopkins, Stanford, and Crocker at Hopkins & Company Hardware (54 K Street, second floor) took business from the steamships, especially after the Central Pacific ate up the Western Pacific, San Joaquin Valley, San Francisco, California and Oregon, Oakland, and Alameda Railroads, but not before men lost their lives in a series of boiler accidents—including the *Fawn*, the *Washoe*, the *Yosemite*, and the *J.A. McClelland*—on the rivers. The *George Washington* did not explode, but she ran afoul and sank above

Vernon of all places.

The railroads nearly put the stage lines out of business too; those that survived, including Wells Fargo, which transported gold sifted, hosed, and hacked out of the Sierras, were consolidated under the California Stage Company by 1853. By the late 1880s, eighty-two people owned a quarter of the best cropland in the Sacramento Valley, one million fertile acres in all. By 1987, the Union Pacific would buy out and kill the Sacramento Northern Railway, one of the most successful interurban electric trains ever to run.

Sacramento's name recalls the story of the Last Supper: "Take eat, this is my body....drink, this is my blood poured out for you..." Sutter was the first to grow wheat and wine grapes here, but after him came distilleries, flour mills, and, north of the city, vast fields of wheat. The armies of reapers that harvested it fed themselves by roasting chunks of bull meat while gathering around a fire. Due to a shortage of fine cloth, flour had to be passed through gauze, producing a cracker-like wafer when baked. Coopers crafted casks, barrels, buckets, hogsheads, puncheons, butts, and tubs. In 1889 believers built the Cathedral of the Blessed Sacrament one block from where the Capitol now stands. Today, a mural on the side of The Bread Store on J Street depicts patrons breaking out of one wall.

This sacramental thematic occasionally leaked out of the city and its county. In 1850, for example, Marysville was named after a survivor of the cannibalistic Donner Party. When Yolo City (now Woodland) was founded nineteen miles west of Sacramento in 1853, a bartender's cursing gave it a nickname: "By Hell!"

IF SACRAMENTO'S SHAPE AND situation suggest an alchemical vas, the operation dominant therein once went by the alchemical term *mortificatio*. After the material worked on with such patient labor decomposes, decays, and dies, it either rejuvenates or must be thrown out. The glum tone of this necessary deterioration characterizes much of the work of Sacramento native Joan Didion, who wrote that her childhood in the culturally insulated city was "suffused with the conviction that we had long outlived our finest hour."

Those words passed through my mind as we stood a block north of the Capitol gazing at what seemed at first like two piles of rubble in front of the Sacramento Convention Center. We had walked here past other provocative artwork, including a bronze Buddha without arms and an orange coyote in a yellow jacket striding across a strip of concrete as though he owned it. The inscription next to the Buddha read, in part,

MY HEART IS ALSO EMPTY
EMPTY LIKE A DEEP WELL
THERE IS ONLY WATER ON THE BOTTOM OF
THE WELL....
THE WATER WILL NEVER DRY UP.
YOU LOOK AT ME UP THERE
ON THE MOUTH OF THE WELL
YOU SEE ME, I SEE YOU TOO.

—as though the site itself were speaking. The coyote came with no inscription, but the Maidu who lived here long before the Americans came told stories of Coyote, who created all things alongside Earthmaker. "Let us two gamble for the world," Coyote said to his companion, who wanted their creation to be good. "I, Coyote, going along in this world, will ruin it."

We had also passed a corner on which stood a street lamp wrapped in green ribbon and surrounded by candles in small glass containers next to pots of yellow, white, and pink flowers. Black and green balloons clung to the pole. Next to it, a mother and brother in mourning had written messages in black ink across a gray utility box: "I love you Mikey! Never forgotten. Sleep tight until we see you again. R.I.P." Coyote had brought death into the world, only to regret it when his own son perished.

The art in front of the Convention Center resembled a set of giant statues tumbled down and broken in two square fountains. In them lay heads, arms, legs, hands, feet, torsos, and faces, some smiling, some angry, others terrified. This was *Time to Cast Away Stones*, 1999, by Stephen Kaltenbach. The title came from Ecclesiastes:

"A time to cast away stones, and a time to gather stones together; a time to embrace, and a time to refrain from embracing...." Words carved into the base of one fountain asked: WHERE ARE WE GOING? At the base of its counterpart: WHAT HAVE WE THOUGHT? On the other side: WHAT HAVE WE WROUGHT? WHERE ARE WE GOING? Another title occurred to me then, that of Nietzsche's book *Twilight of the Idols*. Kaltenbach's painting *Portrait of My Father* hung in the Crocker Museum and reminded Lial Jones, its director, of mortality.

Mortality haunts Capitol Park and its profusion of memorials planted behind the Capitol, in the zone, so to speak, of its geographic unconscious. We strolled by commemorations of firefighters, Union veterans of the Civil War, California pioneers, September 11 victims, Native Americans, Hispanics, and even Junípero Serra, who "brought civilization to our land." A metallic likeness of that land lay at his feet. Someone had placed a fading red blossom on San Diego. Within the circle of the Vietnam Veterans Memorial the likeness of a field medic stood over the likeness of a soldier missing an arm. Even the exhibit's plaque had been dismembered.

In his insightful paper "Mourning and Melancholia" Freud observed the connection between mourning and maturation. To be unable to mourn a loss is to remain, he noted, fixated on the lost loved one. In *The Soul in Grief*, psychologist Robert Romanyshyn tells of how he tried to repair a bookshelf that held writings by himself and his recently deceased wife. The shelf kept breaking, so he finally decided to let it stay that way. This decision hurt, but he needed it. To move beyond denial, false cheer, cynical neurasthenia, or manic images of progress like those of men plowing, hiking, and hammering on the sides of government buildings around the Capitol and into mourning for that which has been lost allows a gradual deepening of self and soul, of reflection and dream, of intentionality and aspiration, that carries the mourner forward into life once again. Only then can our ghosts (as psychoanalyst Christopher Bollas pointed out) turn into ancestors. We must turn toward the dead to be free of them, and perhaps for them to be free of us.

Perhaps the controlling, the manic, and the neurasthenic have flocked to this place because of an unconscious need to mourn.

When settlers first arrived in the Sacramento Valley, the native people already here pointed in warning at the strange white rings high
up on the trunks of trees. For most of its hundred-and-fifty-mile
length and forty-mile width, the valley was a silty floodplain swept
by cycles of *solutio*.

No matter, replied the settlers. Wasn't life itself a gamble?
Besides, Brannan's *California Star*, the *Placer Times*, and other newspapers funded by unscrupulous realtors and speculators gave bland
assurance that Sacramento could be protected easily from any
flooding, easily, yes, and at minimal cost, too. Meanwhile, riparian
forests that had dispersed running water and kept soil from eroding
were fed into sawmills and steamboat engines. Colonies that would
have been called fiefdoms in another age raised levees, bypasses,
canals, and weirs to push unwanted water toward neighbors who
responded in kind. Debris from mining collected on river bottoms.

The rivers rose in the spring of 1840. The eco-baptismal floods of
1849 and 1850, years in which Sacramento vied to become the state
capital, washed away levees (defenses against sorrow and *solutio*?),
houses, ranches, businesses, and cattle. Some men stole a boat in
lieu of unpaid back wages; boats were going for $1,000 apiece while
the flooding lasted. To ferry a lady from up town to Second and L
paid $35. A "Tent City" set up on high ground enclosed a full third
of the city's population. The tent city returns whenever the numbers of Sacramento homeless multiply.

From 1852 floods of currency, newcomers, and rivers continued
to rise. In December 1861 much of the Central Valley flooded, temporarily resuming its previous oceanic state. By 1862, another well-
soaked year, a letter by Hastings referred to Sacramento as "the
Subterranean City." Again and again the American River washed
away makeshift mining towns. Recently elected state governor
Leland Stanford paddled to the festivities in a rowboat.

> So optimistic were nineteenth-century Californ-
> ians, so assured were they that the environment
> could be manipulated as they wished, that they
> went on proclaiming their confidence to them-

selves decade after decade, despite the repeated failure of their plans and projects. The city of
Sacramento would have to build its levees ever
higher as the years passed and at ever greater cost.

– Robert Kelly

Droughts often followed the floods, as did fires: a September 13th
outbreak in 1849 consumed a stock of hay on K Street. Fires in 1850,
1852, and other years did much more damage. In 1908 the
Sacramento Engine Company No. 1 building burned down. Ex-
miner Samuel Curtis Upham made a recommendation: "The practice
of keeping powder and loaded guns in stores and tents, generally, is
one that requires immediate remedy."

Determined to control the weather instead of adapting to it, the
engineers and financiers of early Sacramento installed levees,
watched them crumble, and built them higher. The year 1854 saw
the first diversion dams on the American River, but the dams stood
on waterlogged clay soil. From 1868-71, when the Green Act handed
almost all of California's wetlands over to private owners, the fiefdoms of the Sacramento Valley doubled as reclamation districts.

As the decades passed and Sacramento grew, efforts at flood control increased in complexity if not in attunement to ecological consequences. The need for irrigation grew once the refrigerated box
car made it possible to ship fruit and vegetables across the nation—
all the way to the East Coast by 1874. In July of 1895, hydroelectric
power from Folsom ran down to Sacramento on the longest trans-
mission line in the world, and in 1907, the Pacific Fruit Express
rolled along in over six thousand refrigerator cars.

Floods and droughts throughout the 1920s convinced the Bureau
of Reclamation to start on what became the Central Valley Project.
California passed the Central Valley Project Act in 1933 so that
bonds could raise the money. As the state and federal governments
tried to figure out who should fund and build what, the Sacramento
Flood Control Project spent $98 million to construct nine hundred
and eighty miles of pumping plants, levees, weirs, canals, bypasses,
bridges, and salmon-killing dams. All this concrete pushed the

floodwaters faster, making them even more dangerous, and left the resulting sprawl and development at the mercy of the elements.

> Fiddling with the variables that control rivers will inevitably produce changes in river behavior that can result in land use problems. This is a point of view significantly different from that held by most hydrologists and engineers, who see a river as a natural resource and hazard whose seemingly capricious behavior needs to be controlled by bigger and better engineering solutions...The geologist sees these solutions as ultimately "temporary" and doomed to eventual failure.
>
> – geologist Jeffrey Mount

By 1967, the Feather River, the last free tributary of the Sacramento, was dammed at Oroville.

When we reached the Capitol Building the front doors were locked even though the place was obviously open for business. Circling around, we found and entered a glass foyer and passed through the metal detectors. I had forgotten to remove the lockblade knife clipped inside my camera bag, but the guards either didn't notice or didn't care.

Once the Americans owned California, statehood required governance. Legislators had Sacramento in mind, but because of the cholera brought by the *New World*, the legislature met in San Jose and emerged flush with drinks, dancing dates, and bags of coins. The legislators met next in Benicia, possibly because the Young Ladies Seminary was there. In 1850 it was Vallejo, now selected as the state capital, but the State House stood unready. In 1851 it was Sacramento at last, a choice made permanent by 1854 when bribery beat the pleas of discarded Benicia. A jail now marks where the legislators met.

Men with shovels broke ground for a new State House in December of 1856, but even then the state found itself in debt and couldn't issue the necessary bonds. The proposed project for a Capitol between I, J, Ninth, and Tenth Streets expired, and the land was deeded back to the city. After four years San Francisco architect Reuben Clark tried again. After designing a Roman Corinthian structure with two wings and a rotunda, he was accused of being a Secessionist sympathizer and of employing Secessionists on the job site. After taking a leave of absence, Clark was committed to an asylum in Stockton in 1866 for "violent outbursts of passion" against his family. Whatever the nature of his illness, he died on July 4th. Construction went forward, with the Capitol finished by 1874.

I stood in the rotunda. A golden ball topped an exterior dome crafted out of copper; the interior dome rose a hundred and twenty-eight feet above me on an iron frame. The double dome elaborated a design by Filippo Brunelleschi, the Italian artist who invented linear perspective in 1418. According to Robert Romanyshyn, this invention, codified by Leon Battista Alberti in 1435-6, represents much more than a new technique of painting; rather, it announces an advancing cultural psychology of distance, disembodiment, fixity, departure, impartiality, dualism, atomism, and onlooking.

> The construction of a linear perspective space is the construction of the appearance of a depth between a distance point and a vanishing point. In principle the degree of this depth is infinite. At the vanishing point the lines of the world converge toward a single dot, a mathematical point where the world itself as texture, quality, and difference begins to fade. And opposite this point, the viewer at the distance point is in principle infinitely far from the world which converges toward disappearance.
>
> – *Technology as Symptom and Dream*

This distancing move away from detail and toward control also left its stamp on the Romanesque buildings after which the Capitol was designed. "Cathedral" means "chair of a bishop," but its height and breadth return to structures designed originally by imperial architects to divide and dominate crowds.

In the center of the rotunda stood *Columbus' Last Appeal to Queen Isabella*, a statue of the queen, her page, and Columbus carved from marble and set here in 1883. The Admiral of the Ocean Sea held a globe in his hand for her cool inspection. After initiating slavery on Hispañola and depriving thousands of native Arawaks of freedom, life and health, he had been hauled back to Spain in chains for acts of gross incompetence that included making false claims to incoming colonists, falsifying his sailing logs, and wrecking the *Santa Maria*. After being allowed another voyage he wrote the Crown to rave about circling around a breast-shaped Earth and locating the Terrestrial Paradise off Venezuela. After that he was finally retired. A younger likeness of him displaying an uncharacteristic pensiveness sat below in the Capitol basement.

We visited the two houses of the Legislature—Senate in the south wing, Assembly in the north—and examined the Great Seal of California above their entrances. On the Seal crouched armored Minerva, the Roman Athena, chosen because the state had sprung from its builders like the goddess from the head of Zeus. Yet don't places somehow name themselves? Maps portrayed California as an island for centuries after it was known to be attached to the mainland. The state is armored in coastal cliffs and inland mountains, both of which resisted colonization. In the sixteenth-century novel *The Exploits of Esplandian*, Queen Calafia, who gave her name to my homeland, was black, wore armor, and commanded the hungry griffins and female warriors that guarded her Isle of California.

We saw murals of presidents and governors hanging above black and white marble floor tiles, Renaissance Revival furniture, light fixtures simulating gas lamps, and California Grizzly heads protruding from lacquered banisters. The bears had been extinct since 1922, when hunters shot the last one in Tulare County. The Capitol cafe displayed black-and-white pictures taken by Mexican photographers.

All in all it felt like touring a tastefully decorated stage setting. But as Albert Camus pointed out long ago in *The Myth of Sisyphus*,

It happens that the stage sets collapse. Rising,
streetcar, four hours in the office or the factory,
meal, streetcar, four hours of work, meal, sleep, and
Monday Tuesday Wednesday Thursday Friday and
Saturday according to the same rhythm – this path
is easily followed most of the time. But one day the
"why" arises and everything begins in that weariness tinged with amazement.

Politics in California has often been described as "dysfunction-
al," but that judgment implicitly assumes a politics for the people.
The unvarnished actuality is that California's political system, like
that of the United States, has been run by political, economic, and
social elites from the start. The system was set up by and for the
wealthy, and as such runs relatively well for them.

For example, the winner-take-all plurality rule in the U.S. pre-
vents any real challenge by a third political party by requiring it to
win an election outright. In nations that rely on proportional repre-
sentation, the percentage of seats a party receives in the national legislature lines up with how many votes it gets in an election.
Increasing the number of seats per district allows smaller parties a
chance to win. Not in the U.S., however, and not in California,
where politicians work across party lines to preserve the single-seat
district.

The federal electoral college further dilutes the vote, as does the
"soft money" of legalized laundering for campaign contributions and
the routine if flagrant conflicts of interest. Since 1998, 43% of repre-
sentatives leaving Congress for private life registered to lobby.
Politicians look forward to lucrative positions with the businesses
that buy their votes. In California, where termed out politicians go
straight to work for the firms they favored while in office, biotech
giant Genentech writes talking points for Republicans and
Democrats alike, one blatant example of many.

Californian politics remains instructive as an amplification of
national trends. Here the socioeconomic gap between the top 10%
and the bottom 10% yawns wider than the national average, and

wider than that of any developed nation. By the mid-1990s, when the "three strikes" law doubled the amount of state money spent on prisons, California had fallen far behind in virtually every measure of governance, education, and public service. Today, as twenty-five million Americans go hungry (six million in California), wars for oil consume trillions of dollars, and unemployment and poverty rates soar in the Golden State, the two-thirds requirement for approval of fiscal reform in each of California's legislative houses allows a small bloc of conservatives and their enablers to paralyze any attempt to enact bills to meet basic human needs.

Paralysis does not mean inaction, though. Since 1879 the state constitution has been amended more than five hundred times. The disastrous deregulation of energy that started under Governor Pete Wilson received hardly any debate before going through. The Initiative started during the Progressive Era has been captured by interest groups working through front organizations that hire consultants to collect the thousands of signatures needed within the hundred-and-fifty-day limit. Once passed, an initiative cannot be repealed or amended. Insurance companies routinely use the referendum to defeat regulations that the companies themselves lobbied for in order to "prove" that voters do not want healthcare reform. This kind of institutionalized subversion also strengthens the illusion of widespread buy-in even though half of California's eligible citizens do not vote (of those that do, 70% are white).

These interest groups can also afford television and radio ads well out of reach of the general public, and can spend more on lobbying in California than in any other state: $212 million in 2004 alone. Many of the ads are staged even though they feature real reporters.

> At a stop in Los Angeles to announce construction
> of a hydrogen filling station, Schwarzenegger drove
> a prototype hydrogen Hummer that turned out to
> be inoperable. In San Jose, he grabbed a broom and
> helped a road crew fill a pothole with asphalt to
> symbolize his commitment to repairing California's

transportation infrastructure. The only trouble
was, the pothole was new. It had been dug out by a
crew earlier in the morning so that the governor
could fix it.

– Edgar Kaskla

In a state with thirty-six million people, fewer than one hundred
daily newspapers are left. Five multinationals control the corporate
media in the U.S.: Viacom/CBS, NBC/GE, Disney/ABC,
NewsCorp/Fox, and Time Warner.

Almost all of the state's most profitable corporations—energy
companies, insurance giants, utilities, banks, telecoms, and pharma-
ceuticals—belong to pressure groups like the California
Manufacturers and Technology Association, the Western States
Petroleum Association, and the California Cable and
Telecommunications Association. The Chamber of Commerce
works hard to block climate change legislation that would relieve
the state's oil dependency. Nor is the immense size of California's
prison system accidental given the powerful California Prison
Guards Union. Our thirty-two prisons, the largest such system in
the world next to China and the U.S. itself, cost taxpayers $26,000
a year per inmate not counting medical care. Of two million crimi-
nal cases filed in the state every year, less than 3% make it before a
jury, and of these, 90% end in a guilty plea because so few of the
accused have the means to defend themselves adequately.

The United States is now the third most socioeconomically
unequal industrialized country in the world after Russia and
Mexico. Yet from 2001 to 2004, corporate income rose 369% in
California, where overall personal income averaged less than an 11%
increase. The top 20% here earn half the state's interest income,
more than two-thirds of the interest from dividends, and more than
90% of capital gains. At the same time, 13% of Californians live
below the federal poverty line, 18.5% of children live below it, and
these numbers are growing. Among the top 1% of the wealthy,
income rose 22.6% from 2003 to 2004 alone, with more than a third
of it from investments.

None of this has anything to do with the fluctuations of abstract market forces. Who controls what is determined by growth machines: Kaskla's term for powerful coalitions that generate wealth for themselves by dominating the land and its products. The machinery often works across party lines and their politicized differences of governing philosophy that share underlying assumptions about private ownership of vast public resources.

By 1870, California found itself one of the most urbanized states in the U.S., and by 1900, the leading agricultural state as well. But its form of government had been formed for an agrarian society preparing for small-scale democracy, not large-scale industrialization or corporate capitalism. One would think it obvious that institutions invented in the mid-1800s have no hope of controlling these enormous power coalitions, many internationally based, financed, or outsourced, let alone of administering seven thousand local governments, five thousand special districts, more than a thousand educational districts, four hundred and eighty-one incorporated cities, three hundred and eighty-six redevelopment agencies, seventy-two college districts, and forty-three national parks. Each state senator represents nine hundred thousand Californians—more citizens than each member of Congress represents—and each Assembly member four hundred and fifty thousand. Between 1980 and 2008, the state added ten million to its population. How can fifteen thousand officials elected by dubious tactics possibly provide sufficient service to thirty-six million Californians, 80% of whom live in urban areas?

> A great many of the tensions in California, especially those regarding immigration control, job protection, and economic development, arise in that gap between the new realities and the old institutions and attitudes.
>
> – Peter Schrag

Since the passage of Proposition 13 in 1978, when California's schools were among the best in the nation, more and more cities and counties have found themselves unable to raise tax money to pay for vital services. Police officers, firefighters, and teachers receive layoff notices even as income continues to flow upward.

It wasn't always this dry. Under Governor Pat Brown, money flowed for mental health, police, fire, prisons, schools, transport, and freeways. University education was almost free. But all this made taxes go up, which meant inflation for property owners. Proposition 13 began the steady erosion of state services, with much less money available under Deukmejian, Wilson, and Reagan, who started the current practice of taking it from the already straining budgets of cities and counties now forced to cut their services.

After the Milk and Moscone murders in San Francisco, Dianne Feinstein, Mayor Moscone's successor, restored the at-large supervisorial election system, reinstated a conservative majority, and expedited construction of high-rises by developers. Under both Nixon and Reagan the Fed reduced contributions to the states and their cities. As Reagan pushed deregulation, fragmentation and division spread everywhere in the competition for scarce funds, delighting nobody but big developers and retailers. After Reagan, Wilson promised a balanced budget by taking property taxes from local governments and giving big business a huge tax break. The state economy responded by sagging even further, especially when the end of the Cold War decreased revenue from arms and military bases.

So it has gone. The politics of California are the abyssal, unreliable, stormy politics of an unconsciously enacted flood plain based in Sacramento and ringed by crumbling levees. In his final days as governor, Schwarzenegger, who rode in on narcissistically confident pledges to balance the budget and departed after deep cuts that did nothing of the kind, pushed a deal to sell eleven state complexes—43% of the state's office space—to an investment consortium that refused to disclose who its players were. In contrast to the governor's claim that the sale would staunch California's recurrent debt problem and make $1.3 billion besides, the Legislative Analyst's office predicted a $6 billion cost to tax payers over thirty-five years. The state treasurer and controller denounced the deal as over-the-top cronyism.

> And all the roads jam up with credit
> And there's nothing you can do
> It's all just bits of paper
> Flying away from you...
> This ain't no upwardly mobile freeway
> Oh no, this is the road to Hell

Sacramento had never ceased to grow, but by 2003, its Port, which had opened for business in 1963, faced bankruptcy, prompting a series of real estate sales. In three years it stood $13 million in debt. Since World War II the city economy had depended on war plants and military installations, several of which closed by the eighties and nineties. Some but by no means all of this lost revenue had arrived after 1989 when high-tech firms moved into the valley.

In spite of these and other difficulties, including more freeway-washing floods, affordable real estate for middle-class households and low-income families encouraged many kinds of people to live here, as did employment in state agencies and on college campuses. In 2002 *TIME* named Sacramento America's most diverse city. Beyond the numbers—41% non-Hispanic white, 15.5% Black, 22% Hispanic, 17.5% Asian/Pacific Islander—diversity mixes cultures in the Sacramento Valley's alchemical vas. At William Land Elementary School downtown, teachers are moving toward multiethnic celebrations because of this cultural blending. What does "diversity" mean as a politically correct honoring of foreign foods when mother is Japanese, father is Filipino, grandpa is Korean, and grandma African American? How do you fill out an official form that cannot include your four languages and ten ethnicities? Perhaps what defines the real California of the twenty-first century is a hybrid vigor unconstrained by nineteenth-century oversimplifications.

WE HAD ENCOUNTERED THE ornate unreality of the Capitol, Kathy and I, and endured that of the Governor's Mansion, a deserted

Second Empire Italianate home with thirteen doors, thirteen stairs out front, thirteen-foot ceilings, and thirteen governors and thirteen of their children as previous residents. It looked and felt haunted. Some said it had been built atop an Indian graveyard. The Reagans had been the last to live there.

We had also strolled through the California Military Museum, with its flags, uniforms, and racks of rifles under glass. A "Global Terror Wall of Honor" listed names of young men sacrificed to the cause of affordable petroleum. A mockup of an Iraqi checkpoint included a warning in English and Arabic: STAY BACK 100 METERS OR YOU WILL BE SHOT. Once Kathy returned home she dreamed about boys scarcely out of their teens trying to find their voice and escape from captivity. One stood on a bridge over the Sacramento River. She wrote,

> The road to hell:
> our sacrifice—the sons: young men to the service of
> war and to the violence of society
> the mothers (daughters too) and the Earth Mother:
> sacrificed to industry
> the men who profit from the gains of war and of
> industry: the Devil

"Selling out": a mining term from the days when miners would take money to give up their place in the mail line. Doing this three or four times often proved profitable.

In sharp contrast to the Military Museum, the State Indian Museum felt solid and real. We found it in the shadow of Sutter's Fort. Where else?

Yes, it was a museum, and yes, art and tools were locked in glass cases, but a post-colonial vitality hung in the air, the soft conversations, the intimacy of the dark rafters overhead, and the wall set aside in honor of the Native elders who had made this shrine possible. Eyes that had studied all twenty-one of California's missions were relieved to see photographs of dignified aboriginal Americans with names and histories intact instead of forgotten. One corner celebrated the legacy and tragedy of Ishi, last of the Yana people. A sign informed me that the Pomo had been California's primary makers and traders of dentalium currency. Evidently they had balanced their budget.

Around carefully preserved baskets danced the distinctive Maidu diamond pattern. Basketry had been a high art in California before castles had risen in Europe. Woven from willow shoots, grasses, and colorful bird feathers, these works of Indian art could hold boiling water, sift acorn powder, cook food, store ceremonial items, cradle infants, gather seed, scoop fish from rivers. When flipped over they could be drummed on. Women wove them with an art now being revived and taught. The regional elaborations of these designs had never ceased.

I spoke for a few minutes with a Navajo docent in her seventies about the need to preserve Native languages, revive the arts, fight for tribal recognition that not all California Natives enjoy. A booming sound gave me a moment's pause as a cannon went off at the fort.

I left the museum more hopeful than I'd felt since coming to Sacramento. Preservation and elaboration of culture dreamed onward; ghosts allowed to soften into ancestors. What better revolt against the mortifying forces of dying empires. If you can't beat 'em, outlast and outgrow 'em. As Native poet Deborah Miranda explains, "Indians evolve like everyone else... We grow into what comes next."

> My father opens a map of California—
> traces mountain ranges, rivers, county borders
> like family bloodlines. Tuolomne,
> Salinas, Los Angeles, Paso Robles,
> Ventura, Santa Barbara, Saticoy,
> Tehachapi....
>
> – from "Indian Cartography" by Deborah Miranda

What comes next always unfolds in the living context of particular places. For its primal inhabitants the land is no backdrop, but an active character in events. "We are California's first people," said the placard in the museum. "Our traditions tell us that we have been here since the beginning." Those unable to accept this because genetic and other evidence seems to indicate otherwise would do well to reflect on the enduring sense of profound emplacement at the heart of this claim that a people and their place are committed permanently to each other.

Gold Country (*citrinitas*)

> "Our gold is not the ordinary gold."
> – ancient alchemical saying

What is gold that we should value it so? Far more than paper currency, more than goods or credit, fame or fashion, sometimes more than life?

The facts surrounding gold like its busy cloud of electrons are easily ascertained. Gold is chemically neutral in its pure form, highly reflective of heat energy, and conducive to electrical flow. Often found with silver, it is malleable, ductile, dense, lustrous, promiscuous in how easily it makes alloys, and imperishable. All the gold ever mined—imagine the holds of one oil tanker filled, or a cube one tennis court long on each side—still circulates. It can be shaped into anything desired, yet it never disappears. A single ounce can be drawn into five miles of wire, or hammered into sheets so thin they pass light, yet unalloyed gold is too soft to build anything. "Gold" in Old English looked like *geolu*, "yellow." "Auric" (containing gold) derives from "aura" and "aurora."

Gold brings a mythology alluring beyond the facts embedded in its shine. King Solomon's Mines. The Golden Fleece. The golden thread of helpful Ariadne. The Golden Apples of the Hesperides, and of Idunn, the goddess who gave youth to her divine family. The Ark of the Covenant, the Seven Cities of Cibola, El Dorado; gold leaf, gold filigree, gold wedding rings, Golden Anniversaries, the Golden Age; the Golden Ratio, Rule, and Mean. Gold Cards and Gold Memberships; the golden haloes of the saints. Neil Young's search for a heart of gold. The Incas, the Egyptians, the ancient Greeks, and the alchemists all associated gold with the sun. Gold, the yellow marker, medal, and symbol of ultimate, eternal value.

Then comes the shadow of this earthly sun: King Midas. The Trojan War, said to be sparked by the golden apple Paris handed Aphrodite, who gave him Helen. The Golden Calf, preeminent symbol of idolatry. Gold cups and bowls for officials entering the Sumerian underworld. The pharaohs of Egypt buried in their gold sandals, rings, and daggers beneath golden shrines. Columbus wrote that gold could help souls into paradise. Before butchering the Aztecs who treated him as an honored guest, Cortés taunted them by claiming that the conquistadors suffered "a disease of the heart" that only gold could cure. The Nisenan Maidu had warned Sutter that gold was bad medicine that belonged to a demon who devoured all who searched for it. Superstitious savages!

Gold, perpetually broke California's state mineral. To announce the news of Gold Rush, Western Union was established, the first step in wiring the entire nation.

> Whether it is Jason in search of the Golden Fleece, the Jews dancing around the golden calf, Croesus fingering his golden coins, Crassus murdered by molten gold poured down his throat, Basil Bulgaroctonus with over two hundred thousand pounds of gold, Pizarro surrounded by gold when slain by his henchmen, Sutter whose millstream launched the California gold rush, or modern leaders such as Charles de Gaulle who deluded themselves with a vision of an economy made stable, sure, and superior by the ownership of gold—they

all had gold, but the gold had them all.

– Peter Bernstein

According to alchemical theory, all metals start out as ordinary or "vulgar" as lead. As the sun, moon, and other celestial bodies pass overhead, their potent sky energies evolve the earthly metals into higher forms like copper, iron, tin, and, eventually, gold. Alchemists believed this because in their view everything grew, even supposedly inanimate matter.

They also believed they could hasten these transformations.

Alchemy in four acts: Blackening, Whitening, Yellowing, and Reddening. Jung tried to squeeze these phases of the opus into a developmental progression of shadow work (*nigredo*), anima/animus work (*albedo*), Wise Old Man/Woman work (*citrinitas*), and Self work unto wholeness (*Rubedo*), a progression literalized and codified by the energetic Jolande Jacobe, analyst-marketer of Jungian psychology. But Jung's own *Red Book* reveals a different order, with imaginal visits by Elijah (Wise Old Man) and Salome (anima) starting off his own "confrontation with the unconscious." Perhaps these four phases have less to do with specifiable archetypes emerging along the way than with the shifting moods of the work.

After the Prime Matter turned black, had been washed white, and had undergone other transmutations—the colorful "Peacock's Tail," for example, and the minor *coniunctio* leading to *mortification*—it yellowed. *Citrinitas* referred to the transmutation of silver (*albedo*) into gold. Its other name, *xanthosis*, is still known to medicine as the discoloration of degenerating, tumorous flesh. "For healthful I can be," warned Mercurius, "and poisonous."

Alchemy has been so thoroughly popularized as a path to self-realization that the popularizers and their audiences often forget that the art and craft of *chrysopoesis* ("gold-making") casts a long, dark shadow throughout much of its many-sided history.

Indeed, most of the alchemists would have laughed at idealization of them and their art. They sought primarily to make gold, and those who couldn't, which was all of them, often faked it. Unaware that true transmutation of elements must be atomic rather than chemical, royal patrons showed their displeasure at being fooled by hanging the offenders from gilded gibbets or exiling them from court. Only for exceptionally philosophical alchemists like Zosimos, Paracelsus, Sir Isaac Newton, and Gerhard Dorn did chrysopoesis represent a path to wisdom.

For the alchemist-miners of the Gold Rush, it meant a chance to get rich quick. This chance had glittered in the ground beneath their boots long before humans walked upright.

At the close of the Permian Period two hundred and fifty-one million years ago, the North American coastline, which began in the middle of Nevada once the Pangaean supercontinent had broken up, was slowly bombarded by a cluster of island arc fragments that fused to the mainland. This Sonomian Terrane thickened to what was to become California, the youngest part of North America, an edge of lithospheric driftwood scraped off the ocean floor by Nevada and, later, assembled by islands just as Montalvo wrote it from fantasy in *The Exploits of Esplandian*.

The third cluster, arriving a hundred and sixty-five million years ago in the middle Jurassic, stretched along a thousand-mile arc known as the Smartville Block. Doubling the width of California, it turned siltstones to slates and sandstones into quartzites. This Block runs under the Valley floor and out to the coast ranges. Its surface wrinkles in an alchemical *massa confusa*; as John McPhee explains, "Yuba City is the county seat of Sutter County, Marysville is the county seat of Yuba County, Auburn is the county seat of Placer County, Placerville is the county seat of El Dorado County, and El Dorado is the county seat of nowhere."

When the Smartville Block arrived, the slow concussions it brought opened faults and gaps through which seawater poured directly into the magma below. There it touched olivine rock flecked with manganese, cobalt, iron, sulfur, and gold. As the heated water leached these metals and rose, seeking vents for a return to the sea, it deposited their sulfides in cooling rock. Brought near the surface, hot gold froze solid (*coagulatio*) in congealing quartz veins.

By fifty million years ago, huge Eocene rivers washed into California from the east, crossing these auriferous beds as they came. Four million years ago the beds began to lift.

The Sierra Nevada ("Snowy Mountains" as the unimaginative Cabrillo named them) wall in the eastern side of the Central Valley to separate California from Nevada. Four hundred miles long and seventy wide, this glacier-polished range of pale granite and dark gabbro receives seventy inches of precipitation a year, most of it snow. Its west side slopes gradually upward; its east drops off, leaving formidable heights once scaled by incoming pioneers, some of whom left their bones in the winter snows.

John Marshall found his fateful nugget of gold in the Sierra foothills five days before the U.S. bought California from Mexico. Few knew at first. Only when Sam Brannan went running around Union Square in San Francisco screaming about the find did the news start to circulate around and outside the Golden State.

The hundred and fifty thousand miners who rushed here from 1849 onward built five thousand miles of ditches and flumes. To draw forth a third of all gold ever mined in the U.S.—enough to allow the Union to sell Civil War bonds to maintain its armies— they washed away thirteen thousand million cubic yards of the Sierras, most of it cannoned away by hydraulic jets that shot water at a hundred and twenty miles per hour. Debris ran brown in once-navigable rivers as Native Californians who had successfully resisted imprisonment in the missions were driven from their homes by miners who stabbed, shot, raped, and scalped their victims wholesale. Bret Harte glamorized the gold-seekers despite having reported honestly about a massacre of Wiyots in Humboldt County. Thoreau denounced the miners as careless, brutal savages.

Before the cannons came, when placer gold was still plentiful enough to find with pan and pickax, miners set up five hundred camps along the rivers branching westward down and across the Sierra foothills. Many of these camps ran along what is now Route 49 curving south to north for three hundred and twenty-six miles like a giant ear surrounding Tahoe: from Mariposa and then Columbia to the south up through Angels Camp (fifty-two miles east of Stockton), Sutter Creek, Placerville (forty-five miles east of Sacramento), Coloma, Auburn, Marysville, Yuba City, Oroville (sixty-nine miles due north of Sacramento), and points further north and east. Chambers of Commerce call this Gold Country and offer tours of what's left of it.

In Mariposa, a former mining camp, this includes a mining museum founded in 1957. On its grounds can be found a gold ore mill, some of John Fremont's furniture, a Miwok hut replica, a saloon replica, and a miner's cabin replica. After Fremont's men had found gold here he had to battle miners in court for his claim. Once the mining died down, tourists taking stage coaches to Yosemite kept the local economy going long enough for the camp to become a town. Fremont, who had been courtmartialed once already, left California, moving on to be relieved of a Civil War command by Lincoln, lose track of Stonewall Jackson in the Shenandoah Valley, unsuccessfully campaign for the U.S. Presidency with the backing of radicals who wanted the South utterly destroyed, and have a railroad repossessed less than a year after purchasing it. He died of peritonitis in New York City, but the little town in California survived him.

As Kathy and I drove north on Route 49 to Angels Camp I wondered why Gold Rush counties were stacked so thickly on top of each other like geologic strata or irregularly shaped earrings crowding a perforated auricle. In biology, differentiation indicates development and specialization; in mineralogy, crystallization; in psychology, material coming to consciousness. The alchemists called this *coagulatio*. What had been rushing to structuralize and complexify? What needed to be heard up here?

IN MARCH OF 1850, Dr. Thaddeus Hildreth, his brother George, John Walker, and other travelers were halted by a rainstorm in what is now Tuolumne County. Walker decided to explore a gulch for gold and found some. In a month, Mexican, Chinese, Irish, Italian, French, German, and Jewish miners were raising tents at Hildreth's Diggins; in a year the Tuolumne County Water Company flumed in water from the Stanislaus River twenty miles away; and in two years the camp had grown into a town called Columbia whose population reached thirty thousand by 1853. A fire a year later burned down the town, prompting citizens to install seven cisterns underground and to rebuild in brick and iron. Rebuilt structures survived another fire in 1857.

By the time we arrived, Columbia had been converted into a State Historic Park. It had been mined out by 1860 with more than $2 billion in mineral wealth taken from the ground (the local Wells Fargo had weighed 1.4 million ounces of gold). The only land left to mine lay in the town itself, so miners dug under buildings and tore down houses to get at the gold. Bricks from the wrecked buildings were transported westward twenty-six miles to Copperopolis. Three miles to the south, Sonora, the county seat, grew into California's second-largest city before the mining mania died down and depopulation set in.

Columbia's main street is closed to traffic but open to pedestrians and horse-drawn carriages. We strolled into the park where more than a hundred movies and television episodes had been filmed, including *The Hazards of Helen*, "California's Gold," *Pale Rider*, and *Back to the Future III*. A docent in the museum—a long wood-beamed room with glass cabinets full of knickknacks and wall exhibits encased in plastic—confirmed that Columbia wasn't really a town anymore, except for some residents at its outskirts.

An antique bowling alley; dry goods; Johnson's Livery ("Horses Bought, Sold, & Traded"); brick buildings, white banisters, red sidings, buckskin leggings. A theater playing *Dracula*; a covered wagon. A wooden sluice where we panned for gold "just like the miners did it," although the gold we sought took more than physical labor to uncover. Freshly painted Columbia should have felt charming, but it was eerily lonely instead. A white-bearded man in a white cap played "Over the Rainbow" on his flute while he leaned against a spindly tree. An upturned hat sat in the street in front of him.

"A stage where nobody lives anymore," I told Kathy as we walked down a trail past boulders twice the size of cars. "A house with all the children gone." As a mother she felt it strongly. Her choice of a black shirt seemed strangely apt. Some of the boulders were pitted where the Indians had ground acorn meal.

A Marble Quarry RV Park sat among stands of stone. Once marble dug from here had surfaced stairways and walkways and hotel facades in San Francisco; today limestone blasted into fragments was trucked out to be aggregate for road work, antacid tablets, and chicken feed. Ten miles northwest of here, enormous limestone caves near Vallecito sobbed whenever dripping water met the wind. For all the next day a haunting, sorrowing emptiness hung around me. Columbia seemed like it had been a nice place to live. Would it be again? *Back to the future,* I thought, summoning the presence of Columbia in my mind's eye. "Colombo," the original version of "Columbus," originally meant "keeper of doves." *Are you destined only to be a stop along the way to elsewhere, your* prima materia *pulverized and scattered across the nation? Or are you a Philosopher's Stone in the rough?*

We were welcomed into Calaveras County by a sign on a rusted mining car filled with rocks. The car stood atop a rock pile. We saw rocks everywhere: in fields, as fences, on hillsides, next to oaks in rolling savannah hills, in gray and orange stands of shale and sandstone. The largest piece of gold found during the Gold Rush showed up here as a two-hundred-pound chunk spotted on Carson Hill. "Calaveras" means "skulls," so named by John Marsh, who saw some around here. In Vallecito, Moaning Cavern still held the remains of prehistoric people whose bones were preserved by mineralized cave water.

Angels Camp began as a trading post set up by shopkeeper and miner Henry Angel. The supply of placer gold that mingled with pyritic fool's gold went quickly, to be replaced by hardrock mining that left the underground riddled with tunnels. Mark Twain lived here briefly before writing "The Celebrated Jumping Frog of Calaveras County," a tale he heard from a drunk miner in a saloon one December evening in 1864. A Jumping Frog Jubilee is still held in honor of Twain's short story. Stony frogs watched our passage through up Route 49 on our way through the boutique town Sutter Creek.

> What you see in Mother Lode towns: retired peo-
> ple; new subdivisions and trailer parks; old frame

houses with clapboards and gable roofs; porches
where old dogs snore; quilts and rocking chairs;
picket fences; taverns with card rooms; museums;
gold samples sold in bottles, as jewelry, and in tiny,
push-lined caskets; ruins; mini-malls; renovated
hotels with flocked wallpaper and an upright piano;
chiropractors and acupuncturists; vineyards; biker
girls in oil-stained jeans; and many images of miners
on signs and on billboards kneeling, panning, or
having a general hoot.

– Bill Barich

As we made for the exit into downtown Placerville, I noticed an
overpass adorned with an inverted V design with the V's interlaced.
There it was again: on the bell tower, on A frame houses in the
forested hills around town, the pointy tops of trees... As we parked,
a figure in a gray-black hooded sweater watched us steadily from
across the street, his face in shadow. I touched my breast where a
pendant hung: Mjollnir, the magic hammer of Thor. I had worn it on
a whim. Was this a place of Odin, said to shapeshift into a cloaked
and hooded human form, his emblem a valknut of inverted V's?

This place had once been Old Dry Diggings. William Daylor and
Perry McCoon of Charles Weber's mining company stumbled upon
it in 1848, and ten thousand miners stumbled in behind them. So did
five outlaws who robbed a French storekeeper in 1849. Three were
wanted already for a murder committed on the Stanislaus River.
Those three were swung from the branches of an oak surrounded by
two thousand miners gathered behind the Jackass Inn. Besides spec-

tacle, one of the unstated goals of summary justice is to prevent deep reflection on the nature of guilt and redemption. Punishment results in a superficial (and juvenile) ritual of wrongs righted but brings no wisdom or healing of the kind attributed to Odin as he hung for nine days from the Norse World Tree. Here in this part of Gold Country the act of ceremonial retribution congealed into a new name for Old Dry Digging, Hangtown, as an ancient mythologem repeated itself unconsciously and therefore without hope of any meaningful transformation.

Nevertheless, buildings sprung up along the creek, in ravines, and on hillsides. One pan of gold from the creek brought a lucky miner seventy-five ounces of gold. A woman out walking found a large nugget and served it to her husband in a frying pan. The names of saloons and casinos might have dropped right out of Norse myth: Boomerang (Thor's lightning hammer always returned to its owner), Trio Hall, Blue Wing Saloon. "Placer" means "sandbank" but also "pleasure."

Steam mills sawed trees as mining camps gave ground to homesteads, mills, and shops. By 1857, Placerville held the county seat of El Dorado and a growing reputation as a commerce route for wagons and carts off to the Comstock mines in Nevada, silver going to the mint in San Francisco, and loads of freight bound for Genoa, Carson City, and Virginia City.

> Few realize that El Dorado was originally a person, not a place. He was said to be the king, or the highest of the high priests, of a South American tribe of Indians, whose city-kingdom was thought to exist somewhere along the Pacific Coast....No one knows exactly how the tales of El Dorado started, but stories about him spread and flourished throughout the Middle Ages. The kingdom that El Dorado ruled was said to be rich beyond mankind's wildest dreams; it had to be, because once a year, at his principal religious festival, El Dorado covered his

naked body completely with a shower of gold dust.

– Stephen Birmingham

Today the creek runs under the town, and its buildings sink slowly into its wellsprings of hidden memory. The stump of the hanging oak, relocated by miners to the Hangtown Bar, is already under the pavement. When millwright George Ranney and wheel-barrow maker John Studebaker removed the tree in 1856, three fires swept the town, some of which was rebuilt in brick. Lightning fires often blackened the surrounding mountains. A bell tower for use as a fire alarm went up in 1860 at a cost of $380. The streets angled around it in a V shape.

At a hotdog joint called Dirty Dawg's I spotted a Minnesota Vikings sticker on a metal refrigerator and stopped to chat briefly with the patron, an extraverted blond with smoldering eyes, deep cleavage, and a Vikings tattoo on her arm. She had come from Los Angeles and stayed for reasons she still could not explain to herself. "Perhaps," I told Kathy, "this place would be incomplete without the figure of Freya." From the International Order of Old Fellows lodge a stylized eye positioned above three chain links stared down at us. Our reflections looked back from the windows of Raven's Tale Fine Books.

Kathy had learned that Odin had dropped some of the Mead of Poetry in Placerville, where poets reside and the Placerville Arts Association sponsors readings. A middle school takes its name from poet E.A. Markham, Superintendent of Education, who lived and taught in Placerville until 1879. Winners of the Sierra Foothills Poetry Contest often come from here. Streets may sink and memories fade, but verses rise long after the vulgar gold's played out.

> *Gold Mine Found.—In the newly made raceway of the Saw Mill recently erected by Captain Sutter, on the American Fork, gold has been found in considerable quantities. One person brought thirty dollars worth to New Helvetia, gathered there in a short time. California, no doubt, is rich in mineral*

wealth; great chances here for scientific capitalists. Gold has been found in almost every part of the country.

– San Francisco *Californian*, March 15, 1848

Beware the Ides of March. As James Marshall recounted later,

> ...It was a clear, cold morning; I shall never forget
> that morning. As I was taking my usual walk along
> the race, after shutting off the water, my eye was
> caught by a glimpse of something shining in the
> bottom of the ditch. There was about a foot of
> water running there. I reached my hand down and
> picked it up; it made my heart thump for I felt cer-
> tain it was gold. The piece was about half the size
> and of the shape of a pea. Then I saw another piece
> in the water...

Equipment miners bought in San Francisco and Sacramento and carried into the fields on the backs of horses, donkeys, and mules might have come from an alchemical laboratory. The Cradle, the Long Tom, and the sluice box sifted gold from dirt (*distillatio*) at the rate of fifty pans per ten-hour day. The "Raster" (arrastra) crushed quartz to powder that miners rubbed on an earlobe to learn its gold content. Samples were volatilized in a retort or mixed with mercu-ry and squeezed out of a chamois bag, a dangerous practice that left many blind from mercury poisoning. (Not only them: seven thou-sand and six hundred tons of mercury entered the rivers of California during the Gold Rush. An ecological event far from over.) Dry miners called themselves "puffers" when water ran low enough to force them to sift pay dirt by blowing on it. To the philosophical among the alchemists, a "puffer" meant an unscrupulous grasper after vulgar gold.

> Notis: To all and everybody. This is my claim, fifty
> feet on the gulch, cordin' to Clear Creek District

Law, backed up by shot-gun amendments. (signed) Thomas Hall.

Clame Notise. Jim Brown of Missoury takes this ground, jumpers will be shot.

The few who struck it rich quickly lost their fortunes as gold ran through their fingers in saloons and brothels. The majority worked long hours on chilly riverbanks to earn little. Some died of diseases like cholera and even scurvy, a sailor's disease on the inland sea of the Valley. Survivors learned, if nothing else, that the world has a way of turning on those convinced it owes them something. Miner Lewis Gunn wrote,

> We made about half a dollar in the morning, and then we separated to try and find some better place for a day or two. I tried a place by myself but with no success, and this made me thoroughly heartsick. I thought of home, of wife and children, how they used to hang about my neck, and sit on my knees, and laugh and enjoy themselves, and how I used to enjoy myself, and I become homesick....I threw myself on the ground under a tree in the woods and cried.

Driving to Coloma through Sacramento means heading forty-seven miles east on Route 50 past stands of juniper, sycamore, pine, ash, alders, occasional palms, ice plant and ivy between overpasses, then microwave towers, strip malls, storage facilities, office buildings, tracts, motor home lots, and a "New Condos in El Dorado Hills" sign, then red soils, dry grass, and the occasional winter mudslide. From Placerville, the drive is nine miles northwest on windy Route 49.

On our drive up 49 we stopped for a look at Chili Bar, nexus of reckless whitewater rafting, in Marshall Gold Discovery State Historic Park. No rafts or boats sailed by on the American River, but someone had defaced a Park sign to read:

DO WhAT
~~NO BOATING~~
~~TAKE OUTS~~
YOU LiKe

Kathy had camped in and around this place and could testify to its history of disruptive behavior. So could Jordan Fisher Smith, whose book *Nature Noir: A Park Ranger's Patrol in the Sierra* offers examples of violent tourists, amateur miners, dangerous drunks, and shack-dwelling squatters stealing from tourists, committing assaults, brandishing guns, battering spouses, and disturbing the peace with loud camp parties. "Pilgrims" hammered together makeshift gold dredges in a feeble hope for luck. Bodies turned up in shallow graves. In nearby Folsom, site of a prison established in 1880 when the Livermore family donated land in exchange for prisoner labor, Foresthill Bridge had seen repeated suicide jumps, parachuting, hang gliding, and stunt drivers of cars and motorcycles. (According to traditional Nisenan belief, the afterlife awaited on the other side of a narrow bridge.) Passersby throw rocks from the height just to see them fall.

Was this wildness a lingering shadow of the once-wild American River running through here, a relative trickle of its former self that still could flood the bar now and then? Was it a psychic translation of this country's having been warped, twisted, folded, lifted out of an ancient sea, upended, and bent by heat, pressure, lava, mudflows, and volcanic eruptions long ago? Or was this an echo of manic miner madness? At days' end their camps rocked with raucous singing and dancing fueled by alcohol bought or alchemized on the spot from crude stills. Miners who could afford it slept with women they nicknamed "soiled doves." The bears and bulls of Wall Street got their names from camp fights pitting penned grizzlies against bulls with sawed horns. The bears usually won.

Fist fights were always common, of course, but by 1850, when easy placer gold ran out and frustrations rose, the folkmoot-style arrangements drawn by the miners from German and Scandinavian tradition broke down. Stabbings and shootings became so common-place that stepping outside a tent in the morning often revealed a body or two a few paces away.

> On Sundays, while you drink your tanglefoot
> whiskey, you can watch a dog kill a dog, a chicken
> kill a chicken, a man kill a man, a bull kill a bear.
> You can watch Shakespeare. You can visit a "public
> woman." The *Hydraulic Press* for October 30, 1858,
> says, "Nowhere do young men look so old as in
> California." They build white wooden churches
> with steeples.
>
> – John McPhee

Camp sites around us had gone through repeated name changes from the lost Nisenan names to those more recent, each sounding almost like a mythological realm: African Bar, Mormon Ravine, China Bar, Dutch Flat, French Hill, Spanish Dry Diggings. Some names reflected misfortune: Murderer's Bar, Slaughter Ravine, Small Hope Mine, Robber's Roost. Others sounded redemptive, like Honor Camp, Temperance Ravine, and Salvation Ravine.

The State Park offered a reconstruction of Sutter's famous mill, although not in its original spot. After the discovery the south fork of the American River changed course and flowed over where Marshall and his men had stood gaping at their find. We inspected a "California stamp" mill for crushing quartz, an ore car red with rust, a miner's log cabin, and a water cannon of the type that had torn down entire hillsides. A plaque named Coloma "the Golden Stepping Stone," but my legs ached and were very heavy. A tall memorial to John Marshall put him high on a stone-lined pedestal adorned with a shovel, a pickaxe, and a pan. The memorial had cost more than the modest stipend he requested from the State of California shortly before his death. His cabin stood collecting orange and yellow leaves across the path from a Catholic cemetery.

Coloma remains unincorporated. Roughly three hundred people live here, including a few part-time miners who half-heartedly pan the American River. Other residents run the museums, many converted from Gold Rush-era buildings, along with a small theater and a blacksmith shop. It feels like a ghost town, and some say that spirits inhabit the empty and padlocked Vineyard House Mansion, an old four-story Victorian across from a cemetery on a hill overlooking Coloma. According to Kathy, the house's original builder, an unsuccessful Gold Rush miner, had a habit of lying down in open graves. This scared his wife enough that she locked him in a basement where, years later, prisoners about to be hanged were kept. He went blind behind the iron bars and starved himself to death. Her first husband, also a one-time miner, had been arrested for tax evasion and liquor violations and committed suicide in an outhouse.

Coloma, such a quiet Ground Zero now given all that had blasted outward in all directions, from Gold Rush to California's statehood, Union victory, international commerce, and the first great wave of immigration into the Golden State. The displacement and death of thousands of Native Californians, many murdered by miners' guns, knives, and diseases. The replacement of riparian jungles of lush biodiversity with invasive grasses clambering over every available hillside. So much unmourned here and as yet unmemorialized: no wonder ghosts walk the land.

And yet. Coloma, "Queen of the Motherload," yes—and possible home to Freya, Norse goddess of love, beauty, wealth, and erotic diplomacy. In some stories her first husband had been old Odin himself. Her hall in Asgard was Sessrumnir, higher and wider than the ballroom in the Vineyard House, sheathed in gold so bright it awed the dead warriors who arrived there. (Had some flown there from Gold Rush graves that peppered the land around Coloma?) Around her neck hung the golden necklace Brisingamen forged by dwarves she agreed to sleep with. (So many of their human kindred left without finding the treasure they had sought.) Around her neck hung a cloak of feathers brighter and more colorful than any worn by soiled doves.

In other stories Freya's lost husband was Odr, whose name means "frenzy," "possessed," "inspiration," "fury," and "madness." She weeps for him with tears of red gold, presumably of eighteen carats because alloyed with copper of the kind found here and there in copper-gold deposits along the American River and throughout much of Gold Country. Gold and copper: the only two non-white metals. The alchemists linked copper to Venus, Freya's Roman counterpart. Her Greek sister Aphrodite was followed around by doves, a symbol of love as well as peace.

With the mining dwarves paid off or buried and the giants of industry relocated elsewhere, Coloma, whose name is a Nisenan word for "beautiful," feels abandoned but also in ecological recovery: Freya's hall closed for maintenance.

WE FOUND THE GIANTS in Auburn, a confluence of streets and architectural styles populated by giant sculptures (one a Chinese miner wrought by Kenneth Fox out of rebar and concrete) and the giant Foresthill Bridge soaring over seven hundred feet above the confluence of the north and middle forks of the American River. The Bridge was built in the 1970s to straddle a reservoir for a proposed Auburn Dam cancelled when the site revealed a Hel of slit trenches, bore holes, and nine thousand feet of underground tunnels. Past the Confluence, giant malls lined up north of town along Route 49, the usual culprits: U.S. Bank, Denny's, Big 5, all housed in squares high and broad beyond thinkable human proportions. Llorona had struck here in 2009 when, gripped by postpartum psychosis, twenty-seven-year-old Kristina Fuelling drowned her eight-day-old daughter Faith in a sink. The court found her guilty of attempted murder.

In Grass Valley we were greeted by a lot full of tow trucks, five exits, tall trees, orange soil, rows of trailers, and the Empire State Mine Park surrounded by ponderosa pine, invasive vinca, wild blackberry, and a fence of stone dug or blasted from the earth.

After 5.8 million ounces of gold were pulled from here, the soils all around remained contaminated by arsenic. The alchemists used this symbol for the poison:

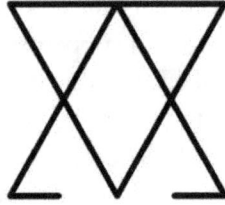

A yellow sign at a branching in the road reminded me of a one-legged descendent of *Jara*, the Norse rune of harvesting the reward of one's labor, but it faced in the wrong direction.

If someone designed this State Park as a graveyard of old mining equipment, they succeeded. Across a gravel field where grass would have grown at Forest Lawn, the machinery was laid out in rows by type—drum hoists, electric motors, water pumps, ore cars, compressors, winches—with little placards to explain the functions once performed. The mine had operated from 1850 to 1956. In addition to tours, period costumes, and mineral samples on display, the Park showed a video about mining: "Tears of the Sun." I was startled to learn that couples got married here.

We entered one of the mine shafts and descended concrete stairs lit by lamps that cast a reddish glow. Cornish laborers had dug, drilled, and blasted their way farther downward. In the 1860s, half died of silicosis, a disease caused by inhaling the dust scattered by air-powered drills. The half that lived shoveled rocky quartz blasted from the walls by dynamite into the waiting ore cars. By the 1900s, manskips carried men down eight thousand feet into three hundred and sixty-seven miles of tunnel. Some of the tunnels flooded despite the steam pumps. A secret room protected by blackout curtains contained a small model for tracking the miners' progress. Most never knew of it.

To finish out this arc of the Gold Country auricle, Kathy drove us northeast along a thirty-two-mile curve up to Malakoff Diggings State Historic Park.

A small town, more a village, had lived here once, but now only a ghost town of white-planked homes and shops dripping snow from their peaked roofs faced the road down which we made our way. This had been North Bloomfield, originally named Humbug by miners less lucky than Roger and Owen McCullough and Owen Marlow, who found gold east of Nevada City in 1851.

The following year miner and engineer Anthony Chabot sewed together a hundred-foot-long, six-inch-diameter hose from strips of saddlebag canvas. Eli Miller, a tin smith, made a three-foot funnel to bring water to their diggings. Edward Matteson joined them early in 1853. Having nearly died while spraying an embankment with water, he suggested attaching a funnel to the front of the hose to wash soil into a sluice box from a safe distance. This worked so well at Virgin Creek that soon eight of these monitors, also known as "giants" and "dictators," fired a hundred thousand gallons per minute day and night into eight miles of sluices and flumes. In 1860 the *Nevada City Transcript* reported that Matteson's labors had "broken into the innermost caves of the gnomes and snatched their imprisoned treasures."

We paused to regard "Giant," a monitor like those whose torrents of water washed gravel, soil, and trees down the hillsides.

> With the invention of water cannons to blast gold out of higher ground away from the river—a process known as hydraulic mining—the Gold Rush became a water rush. Mining and water companies diverted hundreds of streams into ditches cut across the canyon walls to the mines. By 1867 all of the miners' aqueducts in Placer and El Dorado counties, placed end to end, would have stretched from there to Minneapolis. For three decades, hydraulic miners committed mayhem in the Sierra. When it was over 255 million cubic yards of mine wastes and mud had gone down the American River alone, the equivalent of 25 million full-sized semi dump-truck loads.
>
> – Jordan Fisher Smith

Willows, cottonwoods, black oak, Ponderosa pine, Douglas fir, and alders surrounded the trail in the Park on which our boots crunched through frozen mud uphill until a vista opened beyond the trees to reveal what had happened here a century and a half ago.

It was as though a giant hand had pulled back the forested skin of the hills before us to uncover layers of torn red flesh rotted into crusty orange, yellow, and bone-white tissue that would never heal. The bare minarets of stratified rock would have looked normal in the Grand Canyon or the Mojave, but here they testified to hydraulic abuse so severe that not even hardy pines could grow on what was left. I was reminded of mountaintop removal, only here the mountain remained, its miles of stony skeleton laid bare to the eye.

Along the American River the canyon walls had been overgrazed by cattle, mined for limestone, cut for timber, burned repeatedly by fire. Mountain lions, bears, trout, ducks, eagles, grizzlies, deer, condors, otters, and coyotes were exterminated.

> There isn't much left of all the wishes and hopes miners brought to the American River in 1848 and 1849 but a few platforms on the canyon walls and an abiding wildness in the culture of America...Not a bit of gold was found in the footings of those camps. The gold all left here for a bank vault in some faraway city. What remained in these canyons was a certain way of looking at land, waters, and women and a hollow yearning afflicting some members of every generation that neither gold, nor sex, nor wine or whiskey can repair.

No one knows for certain how the Malakoff mine was named, although an article in the *Nevada Democrat* on June 1, 1859 refers to "A. Malakoff and Co." making money on Virgin Creek. The Creek was a virgin no longer. Coincidentally, or synchronistically, many of the French miners who worked there might have been familiar with the battle at Fort Malakov in Russia during the Crimean War. Hydraulic monitors at the mine might have reminded them of the cannons fired at the fort positioned on a high cliff.

From the *Historic Walking Tour* brochure, a leaflet taken from a box on the side of an empty ghost town building:

> A movement from the early sixties created the Park in 1965 to preserve the exciting and controversial history of Hydraulic Mining. Today, this unique and beautiful unit of the California State Park system preserves over 3,000 acres of pine-oak woodland, the eerie but beautiful 600 foot deep hydraulic mining pit, and the remains of formerly vibrant North Bloomfield.
>
> If you listen carefully, you may hear piano music and laughter, the excited shouts of children on their way home from school, horses nickering, and the roar of giant water cannons and shouting miners echo across the gold-laden canyon walls.

The poet Bayard Taylor penned a rather different reaction: "Nature here reminds one of a princess, fallen into the hands of robbers, who cut off her fingers for the sake of the jewels she wears." At the remembrance of his words my heart clenched in pain and anger to see this lingering devastation. California had draped herself in well-moistened forests and covered herself in shining mineral finery. Well worthy of appreciation, she had been brutally assaulted instead by men whose emotional maturity barely matched that of neurotic adolescents. For several moments my clenched jaw made speech impossible. Kathy gazed at the barren hills in matching silence.

In 1884, Judge Lorenzo Sawyer finally outlawed hydraulic mining despite intense political pressure from the mining interests that had benefited from it. After his judgment North Bloomfield emptied, abandoned to nature except for a marshal's office, a barber shop, a grocery, a church, and a saloon preserved for their history. Adept at mining, its citizens evidently lacked the mental flexibility to make a living without destroying their surroundings.

Would any of this ever heal? My eyes searched for something green and hopeful but saw only a moonscape at first. Its cliffs stood over what had been a riverbed but was now a cracked plain occupied only by hardy clumps of scrub.

> The sensation of my skin has supplied me with an illusion of a distinct edge, a definable limit between myself and the world. But it's a false autonomy. I know a woman in these mountains who startled and dropped a dish at the exact moment her husband died in a motorcycle crash, miles away. I know a man who carries the canyons of the American River inside himself, in his blood, in his brain.
>
> – Jordan Fisher Smith

During his stint as a ranger Smith came down with Lyme Disease. It robbed him of thought and memory. But to his surprise, the memories of the American River remained intact. "The other surprise was that as I was healing, the American River's situation had gotten better, too."

The self-realization school of alchemy regards gold as an outward symbol of an imperishable interior reality. Wells Fargo, King Midas, and Croesus & Company hold gold as a precious metal that surpassed any interior values whatsoever in its sky-scraping symbolization of elite financial status. My travels through Gold Country convinced me that the truth of the matter did not lie in between. To reduce gold to a symbol, whether inner or outer, dematerialized sensitivity to deep psychic bonds with the aliveness of the natural world. These bonds could not dissolve, but they do run underground gaining turbulence as they drop.

> Like the treasure troves and gold mines of the Northern dwarves and elves which lie hidden under boulders and beneath the roots of trees, the *lumen naturae*, or natural light, is trapped, as is the

celestial *nous* of Gnostic speculation, in the heaviness of matter itself.

– Greg Mogenson

It is no ecopsychological accident that the destruction spread by mining has increased in step with our perceived distance from a world we are taught to believe is dead and dumb. At an unconscious level below greed or guile, the drills and dynamite, cannons and ore cars scream the same unperceived plea downward into the planet's rocky interior: *Let me in!* But the earthly sentience whose light we long to wrap ourselves in and come home to waits in the depths of self and soil where pick and shovel cannot reach.

Redding (*rubedo*)

> Every true California story, I would learn, begins in
> yearning and ends in transformation.
>
> – Bill Barich

It rained as I entered Yuba City, and the rain followed me all the
way to Redding.

Picture a V, but on top of an I. This, the first modern rendering
of the English letter Y, indicates something of this letter's difficulty
in making up its mind what to be. Vowel, semivowel, consonant, or
diphthong? WY, VI, U, V, Þ, ɨ, or ɛi? Pronounced "why," "ee," "eye,"
"j," "w," "oo," or "th"? The Romans used it to borrow Greek words,
the Anglo Saxons to borrow Latin words, Middle English for "I,"
Caxton to render "th" and "j" in a typeface. The Poles call it by a
French word taken from the Greek. We still use it to turn verbs
(die) into gerunds (dying). The Japanese use it to denote resale
price maintenance, which means forbidding someone to buy from
you and resell high enough to compete with you. In Spanish Y
means "and." The alchemists would have said it means *coniunctio*, a
joining of two substances to make a third. In plumbing, ducting,
and electrical work, a Y joint splits or combines currents or cables.

The letter Y even looks like a funnel.

"Why" goes back to words for "what," "where," and, ultimately, "who."

Why ask Y? Because the Feather and Yuba Rivers join to make a Y-shaped confluence. Yuba City sits under the western arm, South Yuba (unincorporated) under the eastern, and Marysville in the crotch, or, if you prefer, the gateway ("Marysville: Gateway to the Gold Fields" as a road sign announces). All three sites occupy lands formerly known as Sutter's New Helvetia.

Yuba City began as a supply and distribution center for Gold Rush miners, Marysville as a trading post and dock for riverboats full of eager miners heading into the fields. The designers of Marysville dreamed up grand schemes of development as millions in gold filtered from the future city's banks southward to the San Francisco mint, but silt and debris from hydraulic mining raised the riverbeds, blocking boats, and rising waters led to levees, blocking expansion and sealing off the city behind earthen walls. But then Marysville's first European name had been New Mecklenburg: "New Big Castle." Around the castle would rise industries fed by railroads, highways, an airport, and a bus line, prompting the nick-name Hub City.

Yuba City's nickname is Worst Place to Live in America, at least according to author Dave Gilmartin, who ranked fifty of them. His reasons included summer heat, mosquitos, poverty, substandard education, suing TIME Magazine for voicing a similar opinion about the place, being the home of mass murderer Juan Corona (convicted despite badly bungled evidence presented by the prosecution), and casting 63% of its vote for George W. Bush. Only Washington D.C. was a worse place to live. In 1985, Rand McNally rated Yuba City three hundred and twenty-ninth in its listing of the nation's most livable metropolitan areas: dead last. This news gave the mayor a sleepless night, but it also prompted residents to print bumper stickers with slogans like, "Rand McNally Kiss My Atlas" and to burn copies of the almanac. They complained that the evaluators had never fished here—"The shad fight you right up 'til you get them in the net"—but the evaluators had never even visited. Their choice for Number One was Pittsburgh.

Does something about the place invite being dumped on, like the nuclear-armed B-52 that crashed in 1961? Does it mean anything that the Indian name for the place was pronounced "You boom"? Or that Joseph Ruth, its first surveyor, leveled Maidu burial mounds to lay out the city? Or that by 1852, the town had twenty houses and twelve saloons? Is it a coincidence that the name of Sutter County's—indeed, California's—first large farm was Hock? That the last name of the hop grower whose oppression of workers ignited the Wheatland Riot of 1913 was Durst, past tense of "dare"? That Yuba City's 2011 unemployment rate hovered near 20%

It's important to remember that the city outsiders love to pour scorn on sits in the Sacramento Valley flood plain, as was painfully evident in 1955, 1987, and 1999. Possibly to reframe these events, the city website "Flood Plain Management" section claims that "everyone lives in a flood plain." This claim is borrowed from the National Flood Insurance Program, which is administered by the Federal Emergency Management Agency. This seems to mean that FEMA, made famous for its New Orleans fiasco after Hurricane Katrina struck, the very agency charged with overseeing national emergency relief efforts, believes that everywhere counts as a potential flood plain, including buttes, bluffs, palisades, plateaus, mountain peaks, hilltops, crags, headlands, escarpments, ridges, promontories, mesas, and mounds. This is one borrowing that ought to be reconsidered by Yuba City. Their flood plain, which happens to be a real one with perfectly predictable consequences, is filling with sprawl. Impermeable asphalt known to accelerate storm runoff and erosion is rapidly overtaking former peach orchards.

Having passed over the Yuba River, by this time only a small stream, I was forty miles above Sacramento. Staying on I-99, I continued north past Oroville, where the Feather River had been dammed, to Chico, forty-six miles above Marysville and seventy-three below Redding.

The name tipped me off. Toward the end of the alchemical endeavor, the material being worked on takes on the aspect of the Son or Daughter of the Philosophers. This *Filius Macrocosmi* emerges as an androgynous product of Sol and Luna (or Sulfur and Salt), the King and Queen of alchemy. Their child brings the freshness, newness, and playfulness necessary for the final stages of the opus. One could think of him/her as a baby Philosopher's Stone finally born but requiring further refining.

In Chico the old makes way for the new, or as the motto above the entrance of the Chico State administration building insists, "Today Decides Tomorrow." In Spanish *chico* means "boy." Pioneer John Bidwell, who laid out the town on top of a Maidu village in 1860, liked to name north-south streets after trees. Marie-Louise von Franz links the tree symbol to the *puer aeternus*, the archetypal and redemptive Divine Child, although Jungians sometimes use the term pejoratively to mean a man who never grows up. His feminine counterpart is the *puella aeternus*. When Bidwell named an oak in Bidwell Park after British botanist Sir Joseph Hooker, Hooker thought the tree was nearly two thousand years old. When it split and fell in May of 1977, however, it turned out to be two trees only five to six hundred years old, much younger than expected.

> ...and did they [the Bidwells] think the earth
> was burning up inside
> with wanton love,
> or did they choose to see
> the stars of heaven scattered
> in the field, like eyes, the many eyes
> of God...
> – Gary Thompson, from "Old Cohasset Road"

The *puer* style can be creative, optimistic, inventive, bold, playful, ebullient, and buoyed up on novel ideas, but if ungrounded can be flighty, undecided, self-absorbed, unreflective, and unable to commit. Think of the boyish Mozart, or of Peter Pan—or, in Chico, of the artisanal start-ups downtown that flourish for a time, the celebratory reputation of Chico State (named number one party school by *Playboy* and other magazines), or the Robin Hood mural on the side of Campus Bicycles on West Fourth and Main where a toy

store once stood. A friend who attended the college years ago complained of trouble finding a lover because all the boys wanted to do
was drink beer and play pool. The tallest building in town is
Whitney Dorm.

A profusion of colors catches the eye, leaping from murals and
the fronts of decorated buildings. The city averages ten to fifteen
parades a year not counting the circuses that have visited since
1900. Parking spaces downtown around the city plaza instruct the
driver to back in: regression in the service of sightseeing on the go.
But where there is *puer*, there shall *senex* be found as well, if only in
a muted old man's voice, like the Medicare claims processing center
or the art deco Senator Theater that replaced the Armory in 1927. In
1998 its tower leaned so far over Fifth Street that it had to be
removed. The Phoenix Building at Third and Broadway was once
Toad Hall, but after burning in 1973 it rose from its ashes to house
new shops and restaurants. Other old buildings—the Park Hotel,
the Crocker-Citizens Bank Building, La Grande Hotel, the Sperry
Flour Mill—were demolished to make way for newer and larger
structures. Among the smaller my eye picked out recreation rooms
(Mind Games, The Force). Two old buildings at the former
Diamond Match Company site were burned down by teenagers in
2004.

Divine Children know no time, but at Kendell Hall, a circle of
evergreens oversee a concrete circle bearing two-digit numbers representing a class that buried a time capsule. Another capsule resides
inside the administration building cornerstone on the same campus
as a child development laboratory and, until 1971, an elementary
school. An electric sign that gave accurate time and temperature
was dismantled in the 1990s along Main for noncompliance with
city sign codes. An Absolute Same Day Express does its business on
idyllically named Arcadian Avenue. The arcadian parks and lovely
greenways surrounding Chico breathe their green fragrances of
organic renewal.

REDDING. YOU WERE GOING to insist on having redness in your name no matter what.

After all, you situated yourself atop the red clay soils of Buena Ventura, the land grant owned in 1844 by Major Pierson B. *Reading*, your first settler, a former cotton broker who found gold at Clear Creek and made himself at home at Ball's Ferry. Reading had worked for John Sutter as a clerk and trapper. Grateful citizens called their town Reading, but the railroad and Post Office preferred the name of railroad land agent and amateur naturalist B.B. *Redding*, who had sent a survey crew to lay out a townsite at Poverty Flat in 1872. The crew's foreman had decided on Redding. When the Shasta County seat moved from Shasta (formerly named Reading Springs) to Redding thanks to a fateful decision by Judge Aaron "Billy Goat" Bell, the citizens celebrated by heating anvils red hot.

Reid's Ferry chugged along until 1915. In the waters below, the *Redd* female salmon plants her eggs in nests dug from the suction of her tail pulling at the gravel. In the ground, reddish copper deposits lay on three sides of the city. The first city hall opened at Shasta Market in a two-story red clay building.

And then the red of running blood: that of the Wintu, used by Reading as paid plantation slaves, and spilled in the Battle of Bloody Island and other skirmishes between settlers and Native Californians. "Salmon wars," the Modoc War, Wintu on the west bank of the Sacramento River versus Yana on the east, the "Mad River" between (so the Indians called it), fevers rising at Poverty Flat (so the Indians reported), and Fort Reading built in 1852 as a watchtower. A brush fire burned it down.

Polarized Redding, founded by a slave-driver and named after a student of wildlife and organizer of the State Board of Fish Commissioners. Sited at the top of the Great Central Valley, but halfway between Sacramento and Portland—hence the interest of the Southern Pacific, who built a roundhouse on Poverty Flat in 1872—as well as between California's eastern and western borders. Supporter of the Union, more or less, yet proposed capital for the State of Jefferson and its plans to secede. Botanical gardens and wildlife preservation, yet "An Evening with Sarah Palin" sold out here in 2009. Law-and-order logging and mining town, yet stopover for Black Bart, Rattlesnake Dick, and Sheetiron Jack. A railhead and terminus of freight and stagecoach lines running north, east, and west, yet a point of departure for trains, planes, power (at Volta since 1902; "electron" means "pale gold" + amber), lumber (via the Terry Lumber Company Flume thirty miles long to Bella Vista), tourists, travelers, traders, water, television, radio, and even the starward gaze at the Schreder Planetarium all propagate away from here, where the Sacramento bends and I-5 meets I-99. The alchemical name: *proiectio*. The Stone begins to radiate.

Mineralized Redding, site of *prima materia* on all sides: copper, iron, zinc, cadmium, lead, sulfur, limestone, various acids, and some gold, earning the place the alchemical nickname of Golden Crescent. Also Iron Mountain, the Afterthought Mine, and gravel crushed to fill holes in the streets. Elemental Redding: not only Earth, but Fire through repeated blazes here and in neighboring towns; Water in the Sacramento, the vernal pools nearby, and Whiskeytown sloshed by the lake named after it; and Air, especially in 1908 when two pilots landed on the north end of Court Street. The airship *America* exploded over Redding a year later, but by 1942, a functioning Municipal Airport.

> The Bering Straits migration, Spanish colonization, the fur trade, the gold rush, the Plains farming boom, Mexican emigration, the westward push of the middle class in the 1920s, the World War Two employment boom, the Sun Belt migration, the pursuit of jobs, and the pursuit of variant lifestyles: mobility and the transformation of populations never ceased in Western America.
>
> – Patricia Limerick

When I arrived in Redding I went for a brief tour. The Shasta County health department provided an example of a Peter Ackroyd's "continuity" over time, having begun as Shasta County Hospital (1989) until 1934, when replaced by an almshouse until

1957. The health department building was completed in 1959. I wondered what other new editions of old forms repeated here.

The sun was about to set, but not before highlighting the red downtown: red building faces, red pillars, red awnings, red sheets of paving, the entire Deja Vu restaurant. A red Mustang parked in front of an enormous mural of Mount Shasta on the side of a building topped by dish antennae pointing in all directions. I paused at the mural without quite knowing why.

At a Texaco station where I stopped for gasoline, two middle-aged women in pajamas and slippers busily bought up state lottery tickets. Letting the place take me where it would, I caught impressions of lights on high hills, empty streets, two-story homes, and vacant fields. One-way streets downtown ran as straight as Time's inescapable arrow. Redding was quite spread out, with a wide circle of space between center and periphery. The small street signs were difficult to decipher, faint numerals on a dimly lit clock.

Within my hotel room—red bedspreads, threads in carpet, picture frames, lamp fittings, roof moulding, bathroom floor tiles, drapes—a map of the dial-shaped layout of Redding showed that after sunset I had driven in a counterclockwise circle. My eye drifted to the bedside clock. It kept flashing on and off even after I reset the time.

Yes. The Horae were here regulating the hours named after them. So was their parent, Chronos, Father Time, not to be confused (as he often is) with the Titan Cronus, the Greek Saturn. In old mosaics Chronos goes by the name Aeon or Aion and holds the wheel of the Zodiac. His wife is Ananke, Necessity. Gnostics thought of aeons as emanations that created the cosmos and embodied being. Jung's book *Aion* describes the evolution of the Self, that spark of the divine-within known to alchemists as the Philosopher's Stone.

But the alchemists never thought their Stone to be purely interior.

Planted where the Sacramento River divides Redding like the hands of a clock, Santiago Calatrava's giant Sundial Bridge opened on July 4, 2004 to bridge the three-hundred-acre Turtle Bay Exploration Park growing in the heart of the city. At seven hundred feet long and two hundred and seventeen feet high, the presence of the bridge spans past (the museum, convention center, conventional businesses, railroad exhibit, traffic-cluttered streets south of the span) and future (medicinal, perennial, and botanical gardens to the north). In Turtle Park lay turtle shells shaped like clocks. The *I Ching*, one of the world's oldest books, is said to have derived its hexagrams from the markings on turtle shells heated to serve as oracles. A basic premise for oracular consultation is that everything happening at the moment of the reading happens together as a meaningful unity.

Yet units of time also divide. In Redding, where I found the Yuba Street clock emblem turned upside down, images of linear time struggle with those of cyclical time. The salmon in the Sacramento, the birds in the sanctuary, the turtles in the bay go by rhythms that pulse from the world that evolved all living things, but the big box stores and strip malls invading the city regulate whatever comes under their power by the ticks and tocks that started up in monasteries concerned about regular intervals of prayer.

> The conquest of Western America shapes the present as dramatically—and sometimes as perilously—as the old mines shape the mountainsides. To live with that legacy, contemporary Americans ought to be well informed and well warned about the connections between past and present. But here the peculiar status of Western American history has posed an obstacle to understanding. Americans are left to stumble over—and sometimes into—those connections, caught off guard by the continued vitality of issues widely believed to be dead.
>
> – Patricia Limerick

The idolatry of money, for instance, which we Americans accept as normal no matter how desperately bottom-line-only considerations threaten life on this planet. The Turtle Bay Exploration Park provides an invaluable education for humans about non-human life. From the center of a politically red county based largely on the economics of ranching, mining, and goods transportation, the park strengthens fragile ecosystems, nourishes a variety of bird species, grows native trees and plants, and restores riparian habitat. It hosts herbs and gives children green spaces for exploring the natural world. But because money determines its very existence, the Park must justify itself by emphasizing its economic benefits: the $9.6 million it brings to the county, the two hundred and thirty-three locals it employs, the $3 million in estimated visitor retail purchases, and the $433,000 in revenue for the city every year. It must do this because of never-ending accusations by conservatives that "green" endeavors cost jobs and revenue. Shouldn't conservatives leave something left to conserve? Shouldn't the idolatry of Moloch and his greed and his "too big to fail" giantism be what we expose, challenging it to demonstrate why we should let it exist?

Time is not running out. It's up. We must bridge to live, or dam and die. Redding's emplaced dial points like the salmon's tail to how to cross the next bend in the river: deep transformation of our relation to nature, and of vulgar gold and other minerals into new relationships with the elements; symbolic meaning rejoined to nature's cycles; a change of course in alignment with the vital redness of the earth-rooted heart.

Rubedo, the Reddening, represents the final stage required to birth the Philosopher's Stone, and the clock is a mandala, a circular image of the wholeness brought by completion. But where was the Major Coniunctio to mark the sacred marriage of elements and minerals that brought the opus to its end? Was the Sundial Bridge the conjunction? The freeways and railways meeting here? Male salmon guarding the egg-laying female? The AC/DC of copper-carried power coursing southward from the dynamos at Shasta Dam?

Eleven more miles. I drove north through Shasta Lake, a dilapidated, devitalized town that had withered and never recovered when the railroad bypassed it in favor of Redding. In another few minutes, again at sunset, a fog closing in, I stood six hundred and two feet above the Sacramento River in the exact center of Shasta

Dam, the largest hydroelectric plant in California.

Construction started in 1938. Toyon, the town assembled for the workers and engineers, was named after the local red berries. With a spillway higher than Niagara Falls, the dam had been assembled in fifty-foot blocks checkerboard fashion. The blocks contained six and a half million cubic yards of concrete, twelve million tons of aggregate rock to mix it with, six million and seven hundred thousand barrels of cement, and thirteen thousand tons of reinforced steel. Each turbine required seventy-five tons of water per second to drive it. Many builders were killed or maimed by accidents. Frank Crowe, superintendent of construction, died shortly after completion in December of 1944.

The dam was sold to the public who funded it as inevitable progress on the march, but the real motivations remained political. Building it stopped a dam at Iron Canyon that would have flooded prime agricultural land. The dam also captured runoff from ongoing logging and mining that denuded the surrounding mountains. As a keystone to the Central Valley Project, it funnels thirty inches of rain— eight million acre feet out of the "golden faucet"—down to the Tulare Basin in San Joaquin Valley. Most of the allotted water drawn from the Pit, McCloud, and Sacramento Rivers does not reach struggling family farmers; instead it flows to land owned and operated by Mobil, Chevron, Getty Oil, Shell Oil, Unocal, Tenneco West, Prudential Insurance, Equitable Insurance, Travelers Insurance, Tejon Ranch, Southern Pacific, Blackwell Corporation, and other corporate giants.

> And the big mouth blind beast beggar of a railroad
> bribed
> the government and after a hundred years they're
> still here
> with Standard Oil, Dole, Chiquita, Bangor-Punta,
> people
> that don't live here, multi-nationals, multimillion-
> aires

getting ready to heist the water off Mount Shasta....

– C.W. Moulton, from "Visiting Mussel
Slough Looking at Stones and Clouds"

From the air the dam looks like an enormous bow stringing the Sacramento River as its arrow. Behind it, Shasta Lake undulates along three hundred and sixty-five miles of shoreline.

Here below me sat the massive hermetic seal at the top of the Great Central Valley's alchemical chamber. A chamber plugged at the bottom four hundred miles away at Tejon. IF YOU SEEK THEIR MONUMENT LOOK AROUND YOU a rust-colored his- torical marker had informed me about the pioneers "WHOSE COURAGE TO OVERCOME HARDSHIP OPENED THE WEST, CONVERTING THE WILDERNESS INTO EMPIRE." Those last three words rang through me as I looked down at the foot of the spillway and out at the river meandering away in the fog. Was this, then, the transformational essence of the Valley? A grand scheme for converting wilderness into empire?

As I had walked toward and onto the dam, my sinuses ached with a sudden pressure. Once in the center of the dam I felt so tremendous a sense of falling that I gripped the rail for a moment. From here I could see the dam's rock-covered south slopes, hear the humming turbines converting water into electricity. The lake was low. Wilderness into empire. But what was empire converted into once it ran out of time?

ONCE UPON A TIME the Great Central Valley was an inland sea. Then, during the Tertiary Epoch, it transformed itself into jungle. The Pleistocene Epoch dawned on a Valley of ice, the Paleolithic Era on meadows, woodlands, and marshes patrolled by ground sloths and saber-toothed tigers. Mastodons, rhinos, and tall camels then took the stage, followed by bears, deer, rabbits, antelope, ducks, and geese too numerous to count by the two-leggeds who spread throughout the Valley.

Europeans arriving after the original native people set aside nine million acres in Spanish and, later, Mexican grants averaging fifteen thousand acres a grant. The railroads driven by Americans and ridden by settlers claimed sixteen million acres. The Timber Culture Act, Desert Land Act, and Timber and Stone Act, all passed between 1873 and 1878, furthered land consolidation by favoring capitalized investors. The Wright Act of 1887 paved the way for local irrigation districts whose financial conglomerates ate up water, land, and riparian rights. Cultivated squares dotted the Valley in which riverine vegetation began to vanish rapidly. Cities grew and spread between the squares.

Of four million acres of wetlands once flourishing here, only two hundred and fifty thousand are left, though not for long. The large lakes have been drained and are gone. Alkali flats, grassland prairie, marshlands of tule beds, oxbow lakes, freshwater bogs; willow, oak, cottonwood, sycamore; golden beaver, mink, otter, grizzlies, black bears, salmon and other fish; ducks, geese, swans, cranes: gone or going fast with the rivers all depended on dammed, the valleys exalted, the hills laid low. Eighty percent of pines in Sequoia and Kings Canyon and 90% in Yosemite silently wear the marks of ecological affliction. Only 15% of the Sierras' oldest and largest trees still stand.

Ten million people will live here in a decade or two, assuming they can breathe the air and survive the agricultural runoffs poisoning their wells and aquifers. The heavy machinery paving the way for "development" compacts soil, tears up the surviving vegetation, drives away what animals remain. Plans are being drawn for Sacramento and its surroundings to congeal and coagulate into one mighty metropolis, Fresno's into another.

However, none of this far-reaching transformation wrought by human design has erased the Valley's primal nature, substance, and source whose mineral symbol gradually percolates to the surface of soils under widespread irrigation.

Salt.

Marine deposits ten miles thick in the Valley floor testify to its oceanic origins. The miners along the American River saw them, as did the first climbers of Mt. Diablo. Drivers on 5 and 99 see shimmers of heat that resemble rippling water. And because thick hardpan seals the surface of that floor, agribusinesses have nowhere to flush the salt from increasingly saline soils. Nor is there enough water for that. In fact, considered historically, the twentieth century stands out as one of unusual moisture in the West during a much longer period of normal drought—a drought made warmer by climate instability on a global scale as excess carbon chokes the atmosphere.

By century's end, scientists predict, temperatures in the Central Valley could exceed those of Death Valley. Before then, 90% of the Sierra snow pack will have melted irretrievably away, rendering the Valley unfit for either large-scale agriculture or large-scale inhabitation. By then it will be a flat desert.

The salt, however, was built in from the beginning, and the hardpan below it blocks deep roots, making all cultivated growth here temporary. From sea to marsh to savannah, cropland, and pavement, the Valley all along has sustained a long drying out no irrigation has ever managed to halt.

The alchemical adepts knew their salt well. Salt seasons, fixes, coagulates. It also sterilizes, making way for new cycles of transformation.

Salt is pure, white, immaculate, incorruptible, bitter, oceanic, and stinging in our wounds. Salt connects to Sophia, goddess of wisdom, always hard-earned with much necessary seasoning; to sulfur, the impulsivity, fire, and passion which salt moderates; and to the body of the World Soul. Little wonder Homer and Plato and generations of alchemists regarded salt as a sacred substance. Paracelsus equated salt with soul. Salinity in blood, sweat, tears, urine, semen, and other fluids of fleshly mortality reminds us of our own ultimate origins in the seas of this still-blue planet.

Salt, a child of lethal, unbreathable chlorine and flammable, unstable sodium, reminds us too of bitter lessons, sharp self-accusations, purgations, and pains. It lends these flavor and taste, and, according to James Hillman, turns events into experiences: "Our wounds are salt mines." "When dreams and events do not feel real enough," he adds, "when the uses of the world taste stale, flat and unprofitable, when we feel uncomfortable in community and have lost our personal 'me-ness'—weak, alienated, drifting—then the soul needs salt." Jung remarks, "It is bitter indeed to discover behind one's lofty ideals narrow, fanatical convictions, all the more cherished for that, and behind one's heroic pretensions nothing but crude egotism, infantile greed, and complacency." In Da Vinci's painting of the Last Supper, an overturned salt cellar sits by the right wrist of Judas.

Where sulphuric drives flame forth in willful Promethean recklessness, seasoned salt remains crusty, mordant, and preservative, lingering long enough to concentrate mere memory and happenstance into remembrance. Salt crowns nobility from below: salt of the earth, sitting above the salt, salt sweated into the Valley by generations of farmworkers joining the salt rising from below in mineralized returns of the oppressed.

Too much salt not only fixes but dries out and kills, grounds the birds by sitting on their tails, desiccates what remains stuck in the barren past. Remember Lot's wife.

Salt's uprising leaves the Central Valley roughly thirty to forty years of agriculture. The writing could not be plainer on the alchemical chamber wall.

I asked David Masumoto what he thought of this prediction. The answer to it, he believes, is small-scale farming: organic, thoughtful, water-conserving. He could be right. Permaculture catchment methods have made gardens bloom in deserts. Composting and mycoremediation can convert soils poisoned by toxins into clean, fragrant, productive humus. According to study after study, small-farm communities show higher income, education, standards of living, and employment than those dominated by agribusiness. The schools, parks, small business venues, streets, sidewalks, sewage, and waste disposal are of higher quality. Family farms encourage buying and spending in town, connect farmers to their customers, grow a sense of community in which civic participation and restorative justice can flourish. By contrast, agribusiness often leaves communities with higher poverty, 20-50% unemployment, huge gaps between wealthy and poor, less local money (because it buys its fertilizer, seed, tractors, and irrigation somewhere else), and confinement of education, leisure, and law enforcement to private elites in gated neighborhoods with high fences. The waste, topsoil depletion, chemical pollution, salinization, erosion, compaction, and runoff left behind can only be healed by sustainable methods applied a place at a time.

Redding has produced all these transformations in miniature, from settlement to mining to mini-Gold Rush and on to strip malls and blotches of urbanization; but the arm of its sundial now points beyond all that to a better future in which dwellers remain in dialog with the lands that support them.

Perhaps, if we hear the lessons in salt.

And in the folklore of those who came before and whose descendants remain.

A Yokuts story tells us that

> A traveling husband and wife heard the hoot of an owl while staying in a cave one night. "Use the same call," suggested the wife. "He will come, you can shoot him, and we can eat." The man called, then shot the owl when it appeared. "Do it again," said his wife. He did, killing another owl. "It is enough," he said.
>
> But it wasn't enough for her. "Do it again," she said. "In the morning they will not come. Call more, and we will have plenty of meat." He did, but his arrows ran out. More owls came, and still more. Finally, the owls attacked and killed both the husband and his wife.

Perhaps we can say, "It is enough" in time.

But if we roll the transformational cycle forward, another possibility comes into view. Sea to marsh to savannah to desert to... what?

Whenever it rains hard and long in the Valley, another reminder of its marine origins reappears as the long-drained lakes refill themselves like unwanted reminders of something long forgotten. Global warming will continue raising the sea levels even if our industries halted and retooled themselves "cradle to cradle" tomorrow. Computer projections predict long, salty arms of the sea reaching through the Delta to flood the low-lying regions beyond it. That is what's predictable. What's not are superfloods brought by wild climate fluctuations of the kind that drowned Pakistan and Australia late in 2010. The flood in Australia covered an area the size of Texas. The lag between fossil fuel carbon pumped into the atmosphere and the storms it whips up is roughly thirty years. Today's floods reflect what went into the air in the 1970s. We haven't seen anything yet.

Scientists at the National Weather Service are watching how currents shift in the warming and acidifying oceans around us. The scientists believe that the likelihood is growing of storms that could rain for forty straight days (shades of Noah and the Ark) and drop more than ten inches of rain at a time. The damage inflicted would surpass that of the worst possible earthquake.

If the Central Valley completes its cycle of transformation, the inland sea would fill it again for the first time in human memory. The waters would cover metropolises, croplands, orchards, livestock, salt-choked marshes, and small-scale farms, making no distinctions, favoring no one, and sparing nothing, leaving in their wake only a murky mirror, parody or belated reminder of the depths from which all human consciousness first rose and to which it will return sooner if unseasoned by wisdom than later.

So WHERE IS CALIFORNIA'S *Philosopher's Stone?* I wondered as I drove homeward down I-5.

In Redding I could see its effects all around, from glittering minerals to less tangible emanations. Clocklike, polarized, carmine-soiled Redding also drew believers like a lodestone pulling iron: Baptists in 1889 followed by Mormons, Seventh-Day Adventists, Congregationalists, Lutherans, Unitarians, Christian Scientists,

Jehovah Witnesses, Presbyterians, Methodists, Catholics, Buddhists, Taoists, witches, Ghost Dancers in the Yolla Bolla Mountains to the southwest. Ceremony in Redding donned many masks: those of magicians, clairvoyants, psychics, palmists, even Professor Fait the hypnotist. Vaudeville costumes, parades, "express runners" in uniform...

Did the Stone of the Wise hide under these disguises? Was it behind the tarps hung over porches and windows during the summer? Or in tents erected near the river for a quick change of clothes? Was it under the billowing bed sheet swimsuits worn by women in old photographs? Had it concealed itself behind blackout drapes and curtains during the Second World War, when almost every house in Redding sported a flapping American flag? Was it in the particleboard invented here by the U.S. Plywood Corporation? The local mountain gravel poured over Route 99?

Aphrodite, why did you bring me out here? I had caught your smile all too infrequently across the Valley: in the face of a woman wearing Old Western dress in Modesto (were those gold glints in her hair?); in the sensuous roundness of fruit underground in Fresno; in the fragrance of peaches growing in ordered orchards: you who came from the seas yourself. Did you bring me here to show me how you look out here, or to complain about so seldom being welcome?

> This valley after the storms can be beautiful beyond
> the telling,
> Though our city-folk scorn it, cursing heat in the
> summer and drabness in winter....
> – William Everson, from "San Joaquin"

> The sky is breathing birds this evening,
> breathing them in and out of the light....
> A sunset lass where land is flattest.
> Where can it hide?
> – Kathy Fagan, from "Blue"

It amazes me that your species is the bridge between us and the diatoms. We need you out here, Goddess, in the very center of Calafia! We need you everywhere, in every corner of the world. If we can't learn from you how to appreciate its beauty and thereby transmute our relationship to it, if we can't revel in the delights it offers with such self-less exuberance, if we can't grow up from being exploiters to ardent lovers of it, finally feeling truly at home here, finally belonging, then we are sunk.

The more reflective among the alchemists understood that the content of their work becomes the process by which they work. If the opus keeps its integrity, not only matter and Stone but vessel, laboratory, and alchemist undergo lasting transmutation. Mine had been sparked above the endless panorama of petroleum tankage abroad in darkened Bakersfield.

Upon completing my "soul-seeing" of the coastal King's Highway by reaching the mission at Sonoma, I had finally understood my "personal" story as one small thread in the weave of California's living history, one event in Calafia's ongoing dream. At the moment of that homecoming and conscious belonging, I had wedded my fate to my homeland's. In the Valley I had now learned something else, a geographic extension of what finding my birth families in Hawaii and the Inland Empire had taught me years ago: that I was more than where I came from. That my goals going forward could no longer include a preoccupation with what injured and pathologized California. I was not her servant, but her witness.

As such I recognized that many of the forces laying waste to California originated elsewhere. However necessary, all the talk and thought about digging in and going local missed the transnational scope of the growing threat against health, democracy, and biodiversity. Fattened by decades of financial nourishment paid for so dearly by the land and its occupants, the reach of giants who occupied my homeland and prospered by hollowing out its belly extended around the world. If we were to respond intelligently to the initiatory challenge they posed, we had to think and act outside the bioregions we sought to protect. Enough of letting our occupiers come to us! We had to scout them out and analyze them deeply before they flattened everything of value.

In spite of all I had seen and felt and recorded, I was nagged by the feeling that I had missed what I sought. To console myself I reflected that perhaps the Valley's Gem of the Wise consisted of something less tangible than crops or coal or anything materially detectable. Perhaps the all-healing Philosopher's Stone circulated through possibilities for transmuting our relationship to the natural world. I thought about the Masumoto farm and others I had seen tending the earth instead of sucking the life from it. Or perhaps we find the Stone in the Valley's rich poetry, or in understanding that depth out here is not only "vertical" into the lows or up to the peaks, but also "horizontal" and "ventral" all around in plain sight: depth not only within, but in between. Valley phenomenology horizontal-izes what we glimpse there by bringing what we need to notice into the foreground up close.

In the Valley culture never strays far from the immediacies of place and land. Here more than elsewhere, practices of any sort not tied to the land usually fail. Inner and outer transformation work together or do not work at all.

Perhaps the Stone pulses in the Valley's millennial attempt to alchemize new cultivars of consciousness.

When I got home I found myself glancing disconsolately at notes and photographs and flipping through books on Californian histo-ry, Californian agriculture, and Californian geography and geology. I felt sure I had missed something. An item I had overlooked struck my attention for no reason I could name:

During the Jurassic, the Farallon Plate just east of the Pacific Plate had pushed its bulk under the North American, thereby laying the geologic foundations for the Great Central Valley. The Coast Ranges and the Sierras would not rise for a hundred and fifty mil-lion years. Through subduction, a northern segment of the Farallon, the Juan de Fuca Plate, had also raised the Cascade Range reaching down from British Columbia through Washington and Oregon and on into the northern part of the Golden State.

So what. I closed the books and went to bed. Let my uncon-scious figure it out.

And so, at last, a dream:

> *I am climbing over a pile of stones. When I finally reach the top after so much effort, I see what the pile had hidden from my view: the rising grandeur of Mount Shasta, not distant but giving itself to my senses with such glowing, radiating pre- sentness that I could almost reach out and touch a snowy flank of the sacred mountain.*

My eyes opened and blinked wide in astonishment. I had just received an imaginal greeting from California's Philosopher's Stone.

Bibliography

Ashmore, Lewis. *The Modesto Messiah: The Famous Mail-Order Minister.* Universal Press of Bakersfield, 1977.

Avella, Steven. *Sacramento and the Catholic Church: Shaping a Capital City.* University of Nevada Press, 2008.

Barich, Bill. *Big Dreams: Into the Heart of California.* Pantheon, 1994.

Bernstein, Peter. *The Power of Gold, History of an Obsession.* John Wiley & Sons, 2004.

Birmingham, Stephen. *California Rich: The Lives, the Times, the Scandals and the Fortunes of the Men and Women who made and kept California's Wealth.* Simon and Schuster, 1980.

Black, Edwin. *Internal Combustion: How Corporations and Governments Addicted the World to Oil and Derailed the Alternatives.* Dialog Press, 2008.

Blodget, Rush Maxwell. *Little Dramas of Old Bakersfield.* Carl A. Bundy Quill & Press, 1031.

Booth, Edward, Nopel, John, Johnson, Keith, and Davis, Darcy. *Chico.* Arcadia, 2005.

Bowden, Paula, ed. *The Golden Hub: Sacramento.* 19th Century Books, 2008.

Bower, Tom. *Oil: Money, Politics, and Power in the 21st Century.* Grand Central, 2010.

Brotherton, I.N. *Annals of Stanislaus County, Vol 1.* Western Tanager Press, 1982.

Brewer, Chris: *Historic Kern County, An Illustrated History of Bakersfield and Kern County.* Historical Publishing Network, 2001.

Brunce, Michael. *Coming Clean: Breaking America's Addiction to Oil and Coal.* Sierra Club/Counterpoint, 2010.

Buckley, Christopher, Oliveira, David, and Williams, M.L., eds. *How Much Earth: The Fresno Poets.* The Roundhouse Press, 2001.

Butler, Lisa. "A Short History of Placerville." El Dorado County Historical Museum.

Cabezut-Ortiz, Delores. *Merced County: The Golden Harvest.* Windsor, 1987.

Chalquist, Craig. *Deep California: Images and Ironies of Cross and Sword along El Camino Real.* iUniverse, 2008.

Chalquist, Craig. *Storied Lives: Discovering and Deepening Your Personal Myth.* World Soul Books, 2010.

Chalquist, Craig. *Terrapsychology: Reengaging the Soul of Place.* Spring Journal Books, 2007.

Chalquist, Craig. *The Tears of Llorona: A Californian Odyssey of Myth, Place, and Homecoming.* World Soul Books, 2009.

Colman, Tyler. *Wine Politics: How Governments, Environmentalists, Mobsters, and Critics Influence the Wines We Drink.* University of California, 2008.

Del Castillo, Richard Griswold, and Garcia, Richard A. *Cesar Chavez: A Triumph of Spirit.* University of Oklahoma Press, 1995.

Dubin, Margaret, ed. *The Dirt Is Red Here: Art and Poetry from Native California.* Heyday, 2002.

Dunne, John. *Delano: The Story of the California Grape Strike.* University of California, 1967.

Edinger, Edward. *Anatomy of the Psyche: Alchemical Symbolism in Psychotherapy.* Open Court, 1985.

Eifler, Mark. *Gold Rush Capitalists: Greed and Growth in Sacramento.* University of New Mexico, 2002.

Fabricius, Johannes. *Alchemy: The Medieval Alchemists and Their Royal Art.* Texas Bookman, 1996.

Field, Mona. *California Government and Politics Today.* Pearson Longman, 2009.

Ferriss, Susan, and Sandoval, Ricardo. *The Fight in the Fields: Cesar Chavez and the Farmworkers Movement.* Mariner Books, 1997.

Haslam, Gerald. *The Other California: The Great Central Valley in Life and Letters.* University of Nevada Press, 1994.

Haslam, Gerald, and Houston, James, eds. *California Heartland: Writing from the Great Central Valley.* Capra Press, 1978.

Hardeman, Nicholas. *Harbor of the Heartlands: A History of the Inland Seaport of Stockton, California, from the Gold Rush to 1985.* University of the Pacific, 1986.

Hawkes, Ellen. *Blood & Wine: The Unauthorized Story of the Gallo Wine Empire.* Simon & Schuster, 1993.

Heinberg, Richard. *The Party's Over: Oil, War, and the Fate of Industrial Societies.* New Society, 2005.

Heinberg, Richard. *Peak Everything: Waking Up to the Century of Declines.* New Society, 2010.

Johnson, Stephen, Haslam, Gerald, and Dawson, Robert. *The Great Central Valley: California's Heartland.* University of California, 1993.

Juhasz, Antonia. *The Tyranny of Oil: The World's Most Powerful Industry—and What We Must Do To Stop It*. William Morrow, 2008.

Jung, C.G. *Aion: Researches into the Phenomenology of the Self*. Princeton University Press, 1979.

Jung, C.G. *Alchemical Studies*. Princeton University Press, 1983.

Jung, C.G. *Psychology and Alchemy*. Princeton University Press, 1980.

Kaskla, Edgar. *California Politics: The Fault Lines of Power, Wealth, and Diversity*. CQ Press, 2008.

Kelly, Robert. *Battling the Inland Sea: American Political Culture, Public Policy, and the Sacramento Valley 1850-1986*. University of California, 1989.

Koeppel, Elliot. *Columbia, California: On the Gold Dust Trail*. Malakoff & Co., 2005.

Lawson, John. *Redding & Shasta County: Gateway to the Cascades*. Windsor, 1986.

Patricia Nelson Limerick. *The Legacy of Conquest: The Unbroken Past of the American West*. WW Norton, 1987.

Maass, Peter. *Crude World: The Violent Twilight of Oil*. Vintage, 2010.

Maynard, John. *Bakersfield: A Centennial Portrait*. Cherbo Publishing Group, 1997.

Marlan, Stanton. *Salt and the Alchemical Soul*. Spring, 1995.

Masumoto, David. *Harvest Son: Planting Roots in American Soil*. WW Norton, 1998.

Masumoto, David. *Letters to the Valley: A Harvest of Memories*. Great Valley Books and Heyday, 2004.

Masumoto, David. *Four Seasons in Five Senses: Things Worth Savoring.* WW Norton, 2003.

Mogenson, Greg. *Northern Gnosis: Thor, Balor, and the Volsungs in the Thought of Freud and Jung.* Spring Journal Books, 2005.

Moran, Bruce. *Distilling Knowledge: Alchemy, Chemistry, and the Scientific Revolution.* Harvard University, 2006.

Mount, Jeffrey. *California Rivers and Streams: The Conflict Between Fluvial Process and Land Use.* University of California, 1995.

Osborn, B.G. *Modesto: An Informal History.* iUniverse, 2003.

Pincetl, Stephanie. *Transforming California: A Political History of Land Use and Development.* John Hopkins University, 1999.

Robinson, W.W. *Land in California: The Story of Mission Lands, Ranchos, Squatters, Mining Claims, Railroad Grants, Land Scrip, Homesteads.* University of California, 1948.

Rocca, Al, and the Shasta Historical Society. *Images of America: Redding.* Arcadia, 2002.

Rocca, Al. *Shasta Lake: Boomtowns and the Building of Shasta Dam.* Arcadia, 2002.

Romanyshyn, Robert. *Technology as Symptom and Dream.* Routledge, 1989.

Rose, Gene. *The San Joaquin: A River Betrayed.* Word Dancer Press, 2000.

Rothenberg, Daniel. *With These Hands: The Hidden World of Migrant Farmworkers Today.* University of California, 1998.

Sampson, Anthony. *The Seven Sisters: The Great Oil Companies & The World They Shaped.* PFD, 2009.

Schell, Hal. *Dawdling on the Delta.* Schell Books, 1979.

Schrag, Peter. *California: America's High-Stakes Experiment*. University of California, 2006.

Shenker, Heath, ed. *Picturing California's Other Landscape: The Great Central Valley*. The Hagging Museum and Heyday Books, 1993.

Shipley, William, trans. *The Maidu Indian Myths and Sories of Hanc'Ibyjim*. Heyday, 1991.

Shiva, Vandana. *Soil Not Oil: Environmental Justice in an Age of Climate Crisis*. South End, 2008.

Smith, Jordan. *Nature Noir: A Park Ranger's Patrol in the Sierra*. Mariner Books, 2006.

Smith, Wallace. *Garden of the Sun: A History of the San Joaquin Valley, 1772-1939*. Linden, 2004.

Starr, Kevin. *Coast of Dreams: California on the Edge, 1990-2004*. Alfred Knopf, 2004.

Steinbeck, John. *The Grapes of Wrath*. Penguin, 2006.

Tamminen, Terry. *Live Per Gallon: The True Cost of Our Oil Addiction*. Shearwater, 2008.

Tarbell, Ida. *The History of the Standard Oil Company*. General Books, 2009.

Tatam, Robert, with Myers, Loicy. *Old Times in Stanislaus County: A Journey to the Past*. Highland Publishers, 1994.

Tuccille, Jerome. Gallo Be Thy Name: The Inside Story of How One Family Rose to Dominate the US Wine Market. Phoenix, 2009.

Von Franz, Marie-Louise. *Puer Aeternus: A Psychological Study of the Adult Struggle With the Paradise of Childhood*. Sigo Press, 1997.

Yogi, Stan. *Highway 99: A Literary Journey through California's Great Central Valley*. Heyday Books, 1996.